Collins
revision guides

Total

GC an

burcy

OOV

Published by HarperCollins*Publishers* Ltd
77–85 Fulham Palace Road
London W6 8JB

www.**Collins**Education.com
On-line support for schools and colleges

© HarperCollins*Publishers* 2003

First published 2001
This new edition published 2003

ISBN 0 00 713621 8

10 9 8 7 6 5 4 3

British Library Cataloguing in Publication Data
A catalogue record for this book is available from the British Library.

Edited by Jenny Draine
Production by Jack Murphy
Series design by Sally Boothroyd
Index compiled by Yvonne Dixon
Book design by Ken Vail Graphic Design, Cambridge
Printed and bound in Hong Kong by Printing Express Ltd.

Acknowledgements
The Author and Publishers are grateful to the following for permission to reproduce copyright material:

Photographs
Agence France Press 43
Popperfoto/Reuters 43
Tim Booth Title page, 2, 8, 20, 22, 46, 52, 61, 67

Illustrations
Sally Artz; Roger Bastow; Kathy Baxendale; Harvey Collins; Richard Deverell; Hilary Evans; Gecko Ltd; Sarah Jowsey; Lorna Kent; Joe Little; Nick Ward

Every effort has been made to contact the holders of copyright material, but if any have been inadvertently overlooked, the Publishers will be pleased to make the necessary arrangements at the first opportunity.

Audio CD
The audio CD was recorded at Post Sound Studios and Air-Edel Studio in London and was produced by the Language Production Company with the voices of Claudia Bergthaler, Stephan Grothgar, Olivier Hess, Michael Hulsmann, Philipp Kunze, Birgit Leitner, Sarah Sherborne, Gertrude Thoma, Elisabeth Wellerhaus.

Production by Marie-Thérèse Bougard, Simon Humphries and Charlie Waygood.

Music by Nigel Martinez and Dick Walter.

You might also like to visit:

www.**fireandwater**.com
The book lover's website

CONTENTS AND REVISION PLANNER

On syllabus	Revise again	Revised & understood

GRAMMAR FINDER

Most aspects of grammar are covered in the 13 topic units, but aspects not dealt with in the topic units are covered in the Further grammar section in Unit 18. The chart below shows you all the grammar that is covered in this book and where you will be able to find it.

	UNIT NUMBER(S)	PAGE NUMBER(S)
Nouns	3, 18	17, 129–31
Compound	18	130
Plural	3, 18	17, 130–31
Declension	18	131
Gender	3, 18	17, 129–30
Articles	3, 5, 18	17, 29, 129–30
Definite	3, 5, 8, 18	17, 29, 44, 129–30
Indefinite	1, 3, 5, 8, 18	4, 17, 29, 44, 129–30
Endings	3	17
Cases	5, 9, 18	29, 30, 49, 133–4
Adjectives	8	44
Comparison of	4	23
Possessive	1, 3	4, 17
Superlative of	4	23
Adjective endings	8	44
Adverbs	7	39
Comparison of	4	24
Superlative of	4	24
Adverb phrases	7	39
Hin/her	7	40
Time, Manner, Place	7	39
Pronouns	9, 13	49, 69
Demonstrative	13	69
Direct object	9	49
Indefinite	13	69
Indirect object	9	49
Interrogative	13	69
Reflexive	2, 9	11, 49
Relative	9	50
Subject	9, 18	49, 126

ABOUT THIS BOOK

This book has been structured to help you revise effectively and confidently for your GCSE German exam:

- Vocabulary and grammar revision has been broken down into a number of short revision sessions
- Quick Check yourself questions test your understanding and pinpoint any weaknesses
- Higher Level material is clearly highlighted for ease of revision
- Separate revision sessions cover the four skill areas (Listening, Speaking, Reading and Writing) to improve your exam technique
- Questions to try give you further practice in answering typical exam questions in Listening, Speaking, Reading and Writing.

☀ Vocabulary and grammar revision sessions

The vocabulary you need to know is broken down into 13 topic units. Within each topic, the vocabulary is further divided into two short revision sessions called What you need to know and Higher vocabulary (see 'Foundation and Higher Level material' opposite). You should be able to read through each of these in no more than 15–20 minutes. That is the maximum amount of time that you should spend on revising without taking a short break.

The grammar you need to know is also broken up into short revision sessions called How the grammar works. Any grammar not covered within Units 1–13 can be found in the Further grammar section on pages 126–39, which includes a useful list of all the common verbs you will need to know. The Grammar finder chart on pages vi and vii should help you to find any aspect of grammar quickly and easily.

☀ Check yourself questions

At the end of each topic revision session there are a number of Check yourself questions. When you try to answer these, you will immediately find out whether you have remembered and understood what you have read in the revision session. All the answers are provided at the back of the book (on pages 140–55), along with helpful advice and tips on how to avoid common mistakes.

If you manage to answer all the Check yourself questions for a session correctly, then you can confidently tick off this topic in the box provided in the Contents and revision planner. If many of your answers are incorrect, then you will need to tick the 'Revise again' box to remind yourself to return to this topic later in your revision programme.

☼ Foundation and Higher Level material

You will find everything you need in this book, whether you are revising for the Foundation Tier or the Higher Tier German exam.

Vocabulary that is only needed for the Higher Tier is separated out in the Higher vocabulary topic revision sessions. Any grammar that only applies to Higher Tier is also clearly indicated by a green background and an appropriate stamp in the margin (see right).

☼ Improving your exam technique

Four Exam practice units (Units 14–17) focus on the four skill areas you will be examined on in your German exam: Listening, Speaking, Reading and Writing.

The author, who is an experienced examiner, explains the types of questions you will meet, how to overcome potential problems and how to ensure that you perform as well as you possibly can in your exams.

☼ Questions to try

You are also given the opportunity to answer typical exam questions on the four skill areas in the Questions to try sections, which you will find at the end of the Exam practice units. The CD also ensures that you have lots of practice for your Listening exam.

Answers are given at the back of the book (on pages 156–78) against which you can compare your own answers. There are also Examiner's comments showing what you need to do to score high marks when answering questions in your GCSE German exams, as well as full transcripts for all the recorded material.

Working through the skills revision sessions will give you an excellent grounding in exam technique.

About your GCSE German course

☀ Awarding bodies

- This guide has been produced to help you study and revise for the German exams set by the GCSE awarding bodies of England (AQA [Specifications A and B], Edexcel and OCR) from 2003 onwards.

- Although this guide was written to cover the requirements of all the awarding bodies, it is important that you know the exact requirements of your own exam, particularly the length of the different tests, the nature of the Speaking Test and the rules for Coursework.

☀ Grammar

- The grammatical content of all the GCSE specifications is the same, and is covered in the How the grammar works sections of this book as well as in the Further Grammar section (mainly Higher Level) in Unit 18. The Check yourself questions will help you to practise the use of the relevant grammar points.

☀ Vocabulary

- The core vocabulary printed in the specifications is different for each awarding body, as is the amount of guidance given about Higher Tier vocabulary. No guide can give a comprehensive list of all the words which may appear in any exam paper; however, if you know all the vocabulary in this guide, you are unlikely to come across many unknown words in your exam. However, one of the higher level skills is the ability to deal with words you haven't met before, so the more you know about language patterns in German, and similarities between German and English, the better you'll be able to cope. **You will not be able to refer to a dictionary in any part of the exam, except for Coursework.**

☀ Types of questions

- The Exam practice units include Questions to try, which are examples of the types of questions used by the different awarding bodies. In Listening and Reading, the question types used by the awarding bodies are very similar, and all the questions in this guide will be helpful whichever exam you are doing. The Writing and Speaking questions will also be of value, as there is little variation between the Boards.

- All Speaking Tests involve Role-plays (for Edexcel and OCR these include a Foundation/Higher Role-play done by both Foundation **and** Higher candidates) and a conversation. AQA and OCR also include a prepared Presentation.

☀ Foundation and Higher Tiers

- You will have to decide (in consultation with your teacher) which Tier of each test you will take. You can take a combination (for example, Foundation Writing and Listening, with Higher Reading and Speaking). If you take all four Foundation tests, you can reach a maximum Grade C. If you take two Foundation and two Higher tests, you **could** reach Grade A (and Grade B with three Foundation and only one Higher), but you would have to score **very** high marks in each test to do so. To get an A* you have to do all four Higher tests.

UNIT 1: DIE SCHULE
SCHOOL

What you need to know

Ich besuche eine Gesamtschule.
In der Schule lerne ich Informatik.
Ich finde Erdkunde sehr interessant.
Ich mache gern Biologie.
Ich mag Physik lieber als Musik.
Mein Lieblingsfach ist Chemie.
Ich lerne am liebsten Chemie.
Ich finde Mathe schwer/langweilig.
In Deutsch bin ich eine Eins.
Ich habe die Prüfung bestanden.
Ich bin in Musik durchgefallen.
Wir arbeiten in der Bibliothek.

I go to a comprehensive school.
At school I learn IT.
I find Geography interesting.
I like Biology.
I prefer Physics to Music.

My favourite subject is Chemistry.

I find Maths difficult/boring.
I get top marks in German.
I passed the exam.
I failed (the exam) in Music.
We work in the library.

DIE SCHULFÄCHER

Betriebswirtschaft	Business Studies
Fremdsprache(n)	Foreign Language(s)
Handarbeit/ Nähen	Needlework/ Sewing
Sozialkunde	Social Studies
Technik	Technical Studies
Turnen	Gymnastics
Wirtschaftslehre	Economics

Die Schulroutine

Ich fahre mit dem Rad zur Schule.
Wir haben fünf Unterrichtsstunden
    jeden Tag, drei vor der Pause und
    zwei nach der Pause.
Jede Stunde dauert siebzig Minuten.
Die erste Stunde beginnt um Viertel vor neun.
Die Mittagspause dauert eine Stunde.
In der Mittagspause esse ich
    Butterbrote/warm in der Kantine.
Die Schule ist um 3.30 Uhr aus.
Nach der Schule treibe ich Sport.
Ich bekomme drei Stunden Hausaufgaben.

School routine

I come to school by bike.
We have five lessons each day:
    three before lunch and two after it.

Each lesson lasts 70 minutes.
The first lesson begins at 8.45.
The lunch break is an hour long.
At lunch I eat sandwiches/a hot
    meal in the canteen.
School finishes at 3.30.
I do sport after school.
I get three hours' homework.

DIE NOTEN

1	sehr gut	very good
2	gut	good
3	befriedigend	satisfactory
4	ausreichend	adequate
5	mangelhaft	weak
6	ungenügend	unsatisfactory

Die Schuluniform

Ich trage…
einen grauen Pullover
eine rote Krawatte
eine dunkle Hose/einen dunklen Rock
ein weißes Hemd/eine weiße Bluse

School uniform

I wear…
a grey pullover
a red tie
dark trousers/a dark skirt
a white shirt/a white blouse

DIE ZIMMER

die Aula	hall
das Klassenzimmer	classroom
das Lehrerzimmer	staffroom
die Turnhalle	gym
die Werkstatt	workshop

DIE SCHULEN

der Kindergarten	nursery, kindergarten
die Grundschule	primary school
das Gymnasium	grammar school
die Realschule	type of secondary school
die Hauptschule	secondary modern school

? CHECK YOURSELF QUESTIONS

Q1 How would you say this in German?

A My favourite subject is German.
B I get good marks in Maths.
C We do PE in the gymnasium.
D I come to school by bus every day.
E Each lesson lasts an hour.

Q2 Choose the set of symbols that go with each sentence below.

A Ich bekomme immer gute Noten in Kunst.
B Ich stehe ziemlich schlecht in Naturwissenschaften.
C Ich bin eine Eins in Deutsch.
D Sport macht mir Spaß.
E Am Mittwoch haben wir nach der vierten Stunde Schluss.

Answers are on page 140.

Higher vocabulary

HIGHER

You need to be able to describe your school and your routine in some detail. It is expected that Higher Level candidates will always look for opportunities to express their opinions about what they do. It helps if you are positive, so say what you do like about school and why.

Meine Schule

Meine Lehrer sind in Ordnung, besonders
  der Mathelehrer. Er ist jung und sehr lustig.
Französisch macht mir Spaß, weil wir oft
  Spiele machen.
Ich treibe gern Sport und spiele Fußball/
  Hockey in der Schulmannschaft.
Ich bin ziemlich gut in Kunst,
  weil ich gern zeichne und male.
Naturwissenschaften finde ich schwer, aber
  ich versuche mein Bestes.

My school

My teachers are OK, especially the Maths
  teacher. He is young and very funny.
French is fun because we often play games.

I enjoy sport and play football/hockey for
  the school team.
I'm quite good at Art, because I like
  drawing and painting.
I find Science difficult, but I do my best.

Meine Schulroutine

Ich komme normalerweise zu Fuß in
  die Schule, außer wenn es regnet.
Meine Mutter bringt mich mit dem
  Auto dahin, wenn es regnet.
In der Mittagspause treffe ich mich mit
  Freunden auf dem Schulhof.
Ich lerne Deutsch seit vier Jahren.
Ich mache meine Hausaufgaben, sobald
  ich nach Hause komme.

My school routine

I usually walk to school, except when it rains.

My mother brings me to school when it rains.

At lunchtime I meet my friends in
  the playground.
I've been learning German for four years.
I do my homework as soon as I come home
  from school.

Die Zukunft

Ich möchte in den Sommerferien arbeiten,
  um Geld zu verdienen.
Ich werde im September in die Oberstufe gehen.
Ich werde Deutsch, Geschichte und
  Englisch studieren.
Ich möchte Elektriker(in) werden.
Im Juli werde ich die Schule verlassen und im
  September werde ich die Berufsschule besuchen.
Ich möchte auf die Uni gehen, aber ich weiß
  noch nicht, was ich studieren werde.

Future plans

I would like to work in the summer holidays
  to earn some money.
I shall go into the sixth form in September.
I shall study German, History and English.

I'd like to be an electrician.
I shall leave school in July and go to
  technical college in September.
I'd like to go university but don't yet know
  what I will study.

CHECK YOURSELF QUESTIONS

Q1 How would you say this in German?

A I find Maths boring, but I'm very good at History.
B My brother and I usually come to school by car except when the weather is very good.
C At lunchtime I meet my sister in the dining hall.
D In September I would like to study Music, English and History.
E I would like to be an engineer.

Answers are on page 140.

☼ Possessive adjectives

■ Possessive adjectives look like this:

Singular		Plural	
mein	my	*unser*	our
dein	your (familiar)	*euer*	your (familiar)
Ihr	your (formal/polite)	*Ihr*	your (formal/polite)
sein	his	*ihr*	their
ihr	her		
sein	its		

■ There should be no confusion about which *sein* or *ihr* is being used. Simply look back to see which noun or person it refers to, for example:

*Der Junge hat **seine***   his homework
     Hausaufgaben vergessen.
*Das Kaninchen hat **sein***   its food
     Futter gefressen.

Similarly:

*Die Lehrerin hat **ihren***   her umbrella
     Schirm mitgebracht.
*Die Mädchen haben **ihre***   their bags
     Taschen verloren.

■ Always look carefully at *Ihr* and *ihr*. With a capital letter, it nearly always means 'your', unless it comes at the beginning of a sentence, in which case it could mean 'her', 'their' or 'your'.

■ Unlike the other adjectives you will meet, the possessives follow the pattern of the indefinite article: *ein, eine, ein.*

Case*	Masculine	Feminine	Neuter	Plural
Nominative	*mein Hund*	*meine Katze*	*mein Pferd*	*meine Tiere*
Accusative	*meinen Hund*	*meine Katze*	*mein Pferd*	*meine Tiere*
Genitive	*meines Hundes*	*meiner Katze*	*meines Pferdes*	*meiner Tiere*
Dative	*meinem Hund*	*meiner Katze*	*meinem Pferd*	*meinen Tieren*

*Further explanation of cases and their uses follows in Unit 5.

■ This pattern is easy to follow for *dein* and *sein*, but less so for *ihr, unser, euer*, etc. Just remember to add the same ending to each one, as if it were *mein*. That includes **adding no ending**:

*Mein Hund heißt Kim. Wie heißt **euer** Hund?*
*Ich spiele mit meinen Freunden Tischtennis. Was macht ihr mit **euren** Freunden?*
*Das Zimmer unserer Klasse ist im Erdgeschoss. Wo ist das Zimmer **eurer** Klasse?*

Note that the second e is sometimes omitted from *euer*.

CHECK YOURSELF QUESTIONS

Q1 How would you say this in German?

A What's your sister called?

B I'll bring my brother with me.

C That is my mother's car.

D The girl is going for a walk with her friend.

E Have you forgotten your bags, Mrs Wenzler?

Q2 Correct the errors in the English.

A Sie ist die Schwester meiner Freundin.
She is my sister's friend.

B Meine Freunde sind böse, weil ich unseren Hund nicht finden kann.
My friends are annoyed because I can't find their dog.

C Bitte nehmen Sie ihre Tasche mit und geben Sie sie ihr.
Please take your bag with you and give it to them.

D Die Mädchen haben ihre Mütter im Kaufhaus getroffen.
The girl met her mother in the department store.

Answers are on page 140.

REVISION SESSION I

What you need to know

QUESTIONS/PROMPTS

Wie ist dein/Ihr Haus?
Wie sieht dein/Ihr
  Schlafzimmer aus?
Kannst du deine Wohnung
  beschreiben?
Können Sie Ihre Wohnung
  beschreiben?
Erzähl' mir etwas über dein Haus.
Erzählen Sie mir etwas über
  Ihr Haus.

Ich wohne...

in einem Einfamilienhaus
in einem Doppelhaus
in einem Reihenhaus
in einem Bungalow
in einer Wohnung
auf einem Bauernhof
Das Haus ist ziemlich alt.
Die Wohnung ist relativ modern.

I live...

in a detached house
in a semi-detached house
in a terraced house
in a bungalow
in a flat
on a farm
The house is quite old.
The flat is relatively modern.

Im Wohnzimmer haben wir...

einen Tisch
einen Fernseher
ein Sofa
zwei Sessel

In the living room we have...

a table
a TV
a sofa
two armchairs

In der Küche gibt es...

einen Elektroherd/Gasherd
einen Mikrowellenherd
einen Kühlschrank
eine Waschmaschine
viele Schränke
Wir haben (keine) Zentralheizung.
Wir haben einen großen/kleinen Garten.

In the kitchen there is/are...

an electric/gas cooker
a microwave
a fridge
a washing machine
lots of cupboards
We have (no) central heating.
We have a large/small garden.

Im Garten gibt es...

Gemüse
einige alte Bäume
schöne Blumen
einen Rasen
Meine Eltern arbeiten gern im Garten.
Ich finde das Haus/die Wohnung schön.
Ich habe mein Zimmer selbst
  angestrichen/tapeziert.
Mein Zimmer ist blau angestrichen.

In the garden there is/are...

vegetables
some old trees
lovely flowers
a lawn
My parents enjoy working in the garden.
I like the house/flat.
I painted/papered my room myself.

My room is (painted) blue.

DIE FARBEN

schwarz	gelb	grau
weiß	grün	lila
rot	rosa	orange

MEIN ZIMMER

In meinem Zimmer habe ich...

einige Poster/Bilder

einen Computer   eine Stereoanlage

einen Stuhl

einen Schreibtisch

eine Kommode

einen Fernseher

ein Bett

CHECK YOURSELF QUESTIONS

Q1 How would you say this in German?

A I live in a semi-detached house.

B We have a new kitchen.

C In my room I have a desk and a chair.

D My parents work in the garden.

E We have a sofa and two armchairs in the living room.

Answers are on page 141.

Higher vocabulary

You need to be able to describe your house in a little more detail and to say what you do in each room. In addition you should be able to say something about the daily routine at home, who does what jobs around the house, and most importantly, what you think about it all.

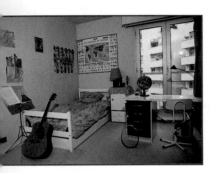

Mein Haus, mein Zimmer

Ich finde unser Wohnzimmer ziemlich gemütlich.
Wir haben ein großes, bequemes
   Sofa und zwei große Sessel.
In der Ecke steht eine moderne Stereoanlage
   mit CD-Spieler.
Wir haben kein Esszimmer und essen fast
   immer in der Küche, die sehr groß ist.
Dort haben wir einen enormen, alten Esstisch.
Ich verbringe ziemlich viel Zeit in meinem Zimmer.
Ich mache dort meine Hausaufgaben, höre
   Musik, lese oder faulenze.
Meine Eltern sagen, es ist immer unordentlich,
   aber das stimmt nicht.
Ich mache mein Bett jeden Morgen.
Ich decke den Tisch und räume nach dem
   Essen ab.
Mein Bruder spült nicht gern.
Ich muss jeden Samstag mein Zimmer
   aufräumen, und im ganzen Haus staubsaugen.

My house, my room

I think our living room is quite cosy.
We have a large comfortable sofa
   and two large armchairs.
In the corner there is a modern hi-fi
   with a CD-player.
We don't have a dining room and almost
   always eat in the kitchen, which is very large.
We have an enormous old dining table there.
I spend quite a lot of time in my bedroom.
I do my homework there, listen to music,
   read or just laze about.
My parents say it's always untidy, but that's
   not true.
I make my bed every morning.
I lay the table and clear away after the meal.

My brother doesn't like washing up.
I have to tidy up my room every Saturday
   and vacuum the whole house.

Meine tägliche Routine

My daily routine

Although this can be a simple list of verbs in the present tense, it becomes much more valuable with the addition of a few extra words, especially time phrases.

Ich stehe normalerweise um 7 Uhr auf.
Ich gehe ins Badezimmer.
Ich wasche mich.
Ich dusche mich.
Ich ziehe mich schnell an.
Ich gehe in die Küche, und ich
   frühstücke mit meiner Schwester.
Ich esse gewöhnlich Toast mit Marmelade und
   trinke eine Tasse Tee oder ein Glas Orangensaft.
Ich packe meine Bücher/Sachen zusammen und
   ich verlasse das Haus so gegen acht Uhr.

I normally get up at 7 o'clock.
I go to the bathroom.
I have a wash.
I have a shower.
I quickly get dressed.
I go into the kitchen and I have my
   breakfast with my sister.
I usually have toast and jam and a cup of
   tea or a glass of orange juice.
I get my books/things together and I leave
   the house at about 8 o'clock.

NOTE: It is better to avoid English names for breakfast cereals and, whatever you do, don't use *Getreide* for 'cereals'.

CHECK YOURSELF QUESTIONS

Q1 How would you say this in German?

   A I think my bedroom is very cosy.

   B Our living room is very cosy, but often untidy.

   C I spend a lot of time in the kitchen, where we also normally eat.

   D I normally get up at around 7 o'clock.

   E I go into the dining room and have breakfast with my father.

Answers are on page 141.

■ How the grammar works ■

☀ Present tense

- It is very important to realise that German has only one form of the present tense, whereas English has three:

  He enjoys school./He is enjoying himself./He does enjoy a good walk.

Regular verbs (also known as weak verbs)

machen to make (known as the infinitive)				Stem	
Singular	1st person	I	*ich*		-e
	2nd person	you (familiar)	*du*		-st
	2nd person	you (formal/polite)	*Sie*		-en
	3rd person	he, she, it	*er, sie, es*	*mach-*	-t
Plural	1st person	we	*wir*		-en
	2nd person	you (familiar)	*ihr*		-t
	2nd person	you (formal/polite)	*Sie*		-en
	3rd person	they	*sie*		-en

- So, if you find yourself writing any part of the verb *sein* and getting stuck for what to write next, look again. If what you are trying to use is the present tense of a verb, one word is all you need. For example:

  I am going   *ich gehe*
  we are sending   *wir senden*

- If you find that the stem ends in a *-t*, *-d* or *-n*, you will need to add an 'e' in the *du*, *er/sie/es* and *ihr* forms:

  Du öffnest die Tür.
  Er arbeitet in der Küche.
  Ihr findet den Film bestimmt gut.

Irregular verbs (also known as strong verbs)

- These verbs follow the regular pattern except in the *du* and *er/sie/es* forms.

  - *Fahren, tragen, schlafen* and some others add an umlaut to these parts:

    du   *fährst, trägst, schläfst*
    er, sie, es *fährt, trägt, schläft*

  - *Lesen, sehen, geben* and some others change their vowel:

    du   *liest, siehst, gibst*
    er, sie, es *liest, sieht, gibt*

- Some of these verbs are very common indeed and must be memorised. A more detailed list of the strong and irregular verbs appears in the Further Grammar section on pages 137–9.

☼ Questions

- The question or interrogative form of the verb is formed by simply turning round the subject and verb:
  Machst du dein Bett jeden Tag?
  Gehen Sie in die Stadt?
  Kommt sie bald nach Hause?

- There will be more notes on interrogatives in Unit 10.

☼ Separable verbs

- Talking about your daily routine means using a number of separable verbs. Remember to take off the separable prefix – that short part at the front of the infinitive – and put it at the end of the clause:
aufstehen	*Ich stehe morgens um sieben Uhr auf.*
einkaufen	*Ich kaufe im Supermarkt ein.*
abwaschen	*Ich wasche immer nach dem Frühstück ab.*

- You will need to use these same verbs in the perfect tense, for example, when you are talking or writing about what happened last weekend. Remember to form the past participle like this:
  Ich bin sehr früh aufgestanden.
  Ich habe in der Stadt eingekauft.
  Ich habe nach dem Mittagessen abgewaschen.

☼ Reflexive verbs

- You will need some of the most common reflexive verbs when talking or writing about your daily routine. You can use them in two different ways, and it is a good idea to decide which you are going to do before the day of the exam!

EITHER:	*Ich wasche mich.*	I wash (myself).
OR:	*Ich wasche mir die Hände.*	I wash my hands.
EITHER:	*Ich kämme mich.*	I comb my hair.
OR:	*Ich kämme mir die Haare.*	I comb my hair.

- Learn to handle the two common verbs which are both reflexive and separable: *sich anziehen* and *sich ausziehen.*
	Ich ziehe mich an/aus.	I get dressed/undressed.
BUT:	*Ich ziehe mir eine Jacke an.*	I put on a jacket.
	Ich ziehe mir die Schuluniform aus.	I take off my school uniform.

  Again, you will need these in the perfect tense:
  Ich habe mich angezogen/ausgezogen.
  Ich habe mir eine Jacke angezogen.

CHECK YOURSELF QUESTIONS

Q1 How would you say this in German?

    A We have a very cosy kitchen, where we always eat.

    B I have a cupboard with lots of cassettes in it.

    C I go into the kitchen and have breakfast with my sister.

    D I usually get up at 6.30.

    E I am putting on my shoes.

Q2 Correct the errors in the English.

    A Wir haben keinen Garten.
       We have a small garden.

    B Zum Frühstück esse ich Toast mit Marmelade.
       I have toast and marmelade for breakfast.

    C Ich verlasse das Haus um halb acht.
       I leave home at half past eight.

    D Ich habe drei Geschwister.
       I have three sisters.

Answers are on page 141.

REVISION SESSION 1

What you need to know

Essen und Trinken

Ich habe (großen) Hunger.
Ich habe Durst.
Ich esse gern...
Ich trinke gern...
Ich esse nicht gern...
Was isst du/trinkst du gern?
Was möchtest du essen/trinken?
Ich möchte...

Food and drink

I'm (very) hungry.
I'm thirsty.
I like (eating)...
I like (drinking)...
I don't like (eating)...
What do you like eating/drinking?
What would you like to eat/drink?
I would like...

Die Getränke / Drinks

Die Getränke	Drinks
der Apfelsaft	apple juice
das Bier	beer
das Cola	cola
die Flasche	bottle
der Kaffee	coffee
der Kakao	chocolate drink
das Kännchen	pot
die Limo(nade)	lemonade
das Mineralwasser	mineral water
der Orangensaft	orange juice
das Pils	lager
der Rotwein	red wine
der Sprudel	sparkling drink
der Tee	tea
der Weißwein	white wine

Das Gemüse / Vegetables

Das Gemüse	Vegetables
die Bratkartoffeln (pl)	fried potatoes
der Kartoffelsalat (e)	potato salad
die Pommes Frites	chips
der Reis	rice
der Salat (e)	salad
die Salzkartoffel (n)	boiled potatoes
das Sauerkraut	pickled cabbage
die Tomate (n)	tomato
der Wurstsalat (e)	sausage salad

Das Essen / Food

Das Essen	Food
der Aufschnitt	cold meat
die Bockwurst (¨e)	frankfurter
das Brathähnchen	roast chicken
die Bratwurst (¨e)	fried sausage
die Currywurst (¨e)	curried sausage
das Ei	egg
der Fisch	fish
das Fleisch	meat
die Gulaschsuppe	goulash soup
das Kotelett (s)	chop, cutlet
die Leberwurst	liver sausage
das Omelett	omelette
das Rindfleisch	beef
das Rührei	scrambled egg
der Schinken	ham
das Schweinefleisch	pork
das Spiegelei	fried egg
das Steak	steak
die Tomatensuppe	tomato soup
das Wiener Schnitzel	veal cutlet in breadcrumbs

Die Nachspeisen / Desserts

Die Nachspeisen	Desserts
der Eisbecher (en)	ice-cream sundae
der Jogurt	yoghurt
das Kompott	stewed fruit
der Obstsalat	fruit salad
der Pudding (s)	instant whip
die Sahne	cream
die Schlagsahne	whipped cream

Das Obst / Fruit

der Apfel (Äpfel)

die Apfelsine (n)

die Banane (n)

die Erdbeere (n)

die Himbeere (n)

die Kirsche (n)

der Pfirsich (e)

die Zitrone (n)

die Traube (n)

(Phrases you will hear in a restaurant)

Ich komme sofort.	I'm just coming/I'm on my way.
Haben Sie schon gewählt?	Have you chosen?
Was möchten Sie?	What would you like?
Sonst noch etwas?	Anything else?
Darf ich … empfehlen?	May I recommend…?
Möchten Sie … probieren?	Would you like to try…?

(Phrases you will need in a restaurant)

Herr Ober! Fräulein!	(to call the waiter or waitress)
Haben Sie einen Tisch frei?	Have you a table free?
Haben Sie einen Tisch für drei/vier?	Have you a table for three/four?
Ich möchte in der Ecke/am Fenster/auf der Terrasse sitzen.	I'd like to sit in the corner/by the window/on the terrace.
Ich möchte die Speisekarte.	I'd like the menu.
Was ist die Tagessuppe?	What is the soup of the day?
Ich bin Vegetarier(in).	I'm a vegetarian.
Ich möchte bestellen, bitte.	I'd like to order, please.
Zweimal Bratwurst mit Pommes Frites.	Sausage and chips twice.
Ich möchte Menü drei.	I'd like set menu 3.
Ich möchte eine kleine Portion…	I'd like a small portion (of…)
Das ist genug, danke./Das reicht, danke.	That's enough, thank you.
Ich nehme als Vorspeise/Nachspeise…	I'll have … as a starter/dessert.
Kann ich Salz und Pfeffer haben?	May I have the salt and pepper?
Das war lecker/prima/ausgezeichnet!	That was delicious/great/excellent!
Das hat sehr gut geschmeckt.	That tasted very good.
Zahlen, bitte!/Die Rechnung, bitte!	The bill, please.
Danke, das stimmt so.	Thank you. Keep the change.
Ist die Mehrwertsteuer/die Bedienung inbegriffen?	Is VAT/service included?

Gesundheit / Health

Mir tut der Finger/das Bein weh.	My finger/leg hurts.
Ich habe mir am Bein/an der Hand weh getan.	I have hurt my leg/my hand.
Ich bin krank/ich fühle mich unwohl.	I'm ill./I don't feel well.
Mir ist heiß/kalt/übel/schwindlig.	I feel hot/cold/sick/dizzy.
Ich habe Kopfschmerzen/Kopfweh.	I have a headache.
Ich habe Ohrenschmerzen/ Zahnschmerzen.	I have ear/toothache.
Ich habe eine Magenverstimmung.	I have a stomach upset.
Ich habe eine Erkältung/einen Schnupfen.	I have a cold.
Ich habe Verstopfung.	I'm constipated.
Ich habe seit zwei Tagen Fieber.	I've had a temperature for two days.
Ich blute.	I'm bleeding.
Kann ich einen Termin haben?	Can I have an appointment?
Haben Sie Tabletten gegen Zahnschmerzen?	Have you any tablets for toothache?
Wie oft muss ich sie einnehmen?	How often must I take them?

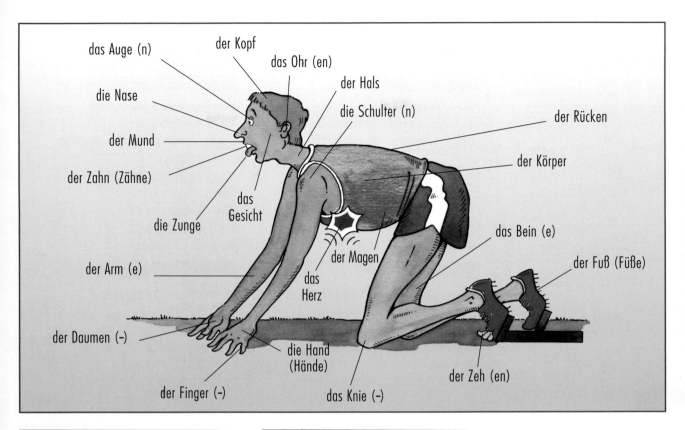

Beim Arzt

Was ist los?/Was haben Sie?
Wie lange haben Sie schon…?
Ich schreibe Ihnen ein Rezept.
Nehmen Sie eine Tablette/einen
   Teelöffel dreimal täglich/vor dem Essen.
Legen Sie sich hin.
Ruhen Sie sich aus.

At the doctor's

What's wrong?
How long have you had…?
I'll give you a prescription.
Take one tablet/one teaspoonful
   three times a day/before a meal.
Lie down.
Have a rest.

CHECK YOURSELF QUESTIONS

Q1 Im Restaurant (Foundation role-play)

  A Ask for a table for six at the window.
  B Ask for the menu.
  C Order sausage and chips twice.
  D Order a glass of white wine and a pot
     of tea.
  E Ask for the bill.

Q2 Beim Arzt

Complete the following interview.

Arzt:	Was fehlt Ihnen?
Patient:	[**A** Tell him you have an upset stomach.]
Arzt:	Wie lange haben Sie das schon?
Patient:	[**B** Tell him for three days.]
Arzt:	Ist Ihnen auch schwindlig?
Patient:	[**C** Say no, but you feel hot.]
Arzt:	Also, ich gebe Ihnen ein Mittel.
Patient:	[**D** Ask how often you must take it.]
Arzt:	Dreimal täglich nach dem Essen.

Answers are on page 142.

Essen / Eating out

Haben Sie reserviert?	Have you made a reservation?
Das haben wir leider nicht mehr da.	We have no more of that.
Geht das zusammen oder getrennt?	Do you want to pay the bill altogether or separately?
Das Glas/Der Teller ist nicht sauber!	The glass/plate is not clean.
Es fehlt ein Löffel.	There's a spoon missing.
Warum dauert es so lange?	Why is it taking so long?
Das Essen ist kalt.	The food is cold.
Die Rechnung stimmt nicht.	The bill is not correct.

Gesundheit / Health

Meinem Freund/Meiner Freundin geht es nicht gut.	My friend is not feeling well.
Er/Sie hat die Grippe.	He/She has the 'flu.
Der Junge/Das Mädchen hat sich am Bein verletzt.	The boy/girl has hurt his/her leg.
Er/Sie ist auf dem Schulhof hingefallen.	He/She fell over in the playground.

? CHECK YOURSELF QUESTIONS

Q1 What would you say to the waiter if you wanted to complain that ...

A ... you have no knife?
B ... your fork is dirty?
C ... your coffee is cold?

At the doctor's or at the hospital how would you explain that ...

D ... your friend has fallen over in the road?
E ... she has hurt her leg?

Answers are on page 142.

☀ How the grammar works

☀ Nouns, articles and genders

■ Unlike English, all German nouns are written with a capital letter, not just the names of people and places (proper nouns). If you don't follow this convention in your writing at Higher Level, you will almost certainly lose some marks.

■ All German nouns are masculine, feminine or neuter:

	Masculine	Feminine	Neuter
Singular	*der Vater* *ein Vater*	*die Mutter* *eine Mutter*	*das Kind* *ein Kind*
Plural	*die Väter*	*die Mütter*	*die Kinder*

■ *Der, die* and *das* are definite articles and mean 'the'. In the plural the word for 'the' is always *die. Ein, eine* and *ein* are indefinite articles and mean 'a' or 'an'. Whenever you come across a new word in German, you need to note its gender and its plural form, so that you will be able to use the word correctly in your work.

☀ Plural nouns

■ All feminine nouns form their plural by adding *-n* or *-en* to the singular. That's the easy part! Most masculine and neuter nouns fall into groups which form their plurals in a similar way, but until you have learnt those you need, it's safer to check them in a text book or dictionary.

■ Most text books show only the plurals of masculine and neuter nouns, but when you find the masculine and neuter nouns in the German–English side of your dictionary, they usually have some more letters in brackets after them:

    Kind (-es, -er)

The first letters are used for the genitive case (more about this in Unit 5); the next letters show you the plural, and it is this which you need to remember.

☀ Article endings

■ It is very useful to remember some other words which follow the same pattern of endings as the definite and indefinite articles. These all follow the pattern of *der, die, das*:

    dieser   this   *jeder*   each, every
    jener   that   *welcher* which?
  Dieser Wagen ist schnell, jener Wagen ist langsamer.
  Jede Mutter mag den Film.
  Welches Kind war das?

■ The possessive adjectives *mein, dein, sein*, etc. follow the pattern of *ein, eine, ein* (see Unit 1), as does the word *kein* which means 'not a' or 'no':
  Ich habe kein Geld.   I have no money./I don't have any money.
  Ich habe keine Bücher.   I have no books./I don't have any books.

Q1 Here are some common examples of words in the plural which you will need. Some of them are rarely seen in the singular. See if you know them already. Some are listed in the singular to jog your memory. Watch out for a few well-known words which are plural in English but singular in German!

Give the German for the following:

Q2 How would you say this is German?

A Which car is faster, this one or that one?
B Every girl likes this pop group.
C I don't like these shoes. Which do you like?
D Everyone knows the answer.

grapes

peas

carrots

potatoes

drinks

trousers

shoes

socks

glasses

buses

school subjects (*das Fach*)

school books

exercise books (*das Heft*)

friends (masc.) (*der Freund*)

friends (fem.) (*die Freundin*)

3 pounds (weight)

2 kilos

teeth

fingers

feet

Answers are on page 143.

REVISION SESSION 1

What you need to know

FAMILIE UND VERWANDTEN

das Baby (s)	baby
das Einzelkind (er)	only child
die (Groß)Eltern (*pl*)	(grand)parents
der/die Erwachsene (n)	adult (*m/f*)
die Frau (en)	woman/wife
der Freund (e)	friend (*m*)
die Freundin (nen)	friend (*f*)
die Geschwister (*pl*)	brothers and sisters
die Großmutter (mütter)	grandmother
der Großvater (väter)	grandfather
der Junge (n)	boy
das Kind (er)	child
die Kusine (n)/die Cousine (n)	cousin (*f*)
die Leute (*pl*)	people
das Mädchen (–)	girl
der Mann (Männer)	man/husband
der Mensch (en)	person
Mutti	mum
der Neffe (n)	nephew
die Nichte (n)	niece
die Person	person
der Sohn (Söhne)	son
die Tochter (Töchter)	daughter
der/die Verwandte (n)	relative
der Vetter (–)/der Cousin (s)	cousin (m)

die Ehefrau (en)	wife
der Ehemann (Ehemänner)	husband
das Ehepaar (e)	married couple
das Geschlecht (er)	sex, gender
der/die Jugendliche (en)	youth/young person
der Schwager	brother-in-law
die Schwägerin	sister-in-law
der Schwiegersohn	son-in-law
die Schwiegertochter	daughter-in-law
der/die Verlobte (n)	fiancé(e)
die Witwe (n)	widow
der Witwer (–)	widower

QUESTIONS/PROMPTS

Wie heißt du?
Wann bist du geboren?
Wann hast du Geburtstag?
Hast du Geschwister?
Wie alt ist er/sie?
Wie sieht er/sie aus?

WIE SIND SIE?

ledig/ verheiratet	single/married
geschieden	divorced
verlobt	engaged
männlich/ weiblich	male/female
allein	alone
arm	poor
böse	angry, naughty
dumm	stupid
faul	lazy
fleißig	hard-working
freundlich	friendly
glücklich	happy
intelligent	intelligent
lustig	cheerful, funny
klug	clever
reich	wealthy
unfreundlich	unfriendly

MEINE FAMILIE

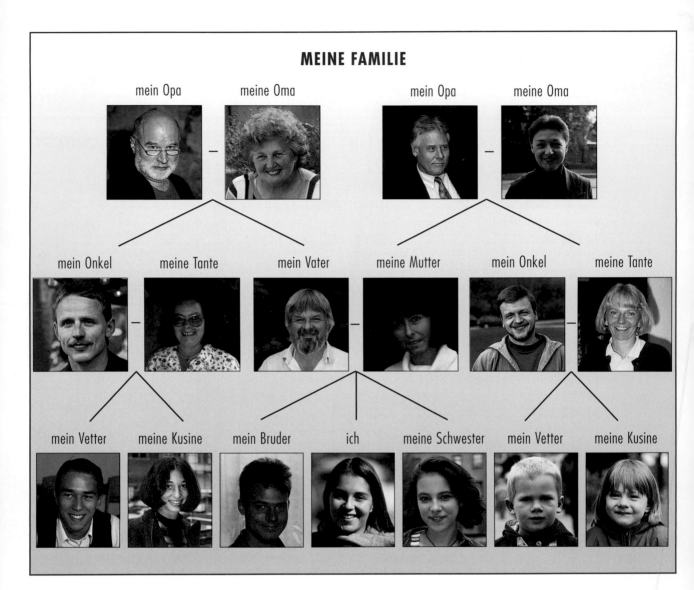

mein Opa — meine Oma mein Opa — meine Oma

mein Onkel — meine Tante mein Vater — meine Mutter mein Onkel — meine Tante

mein Vetter meine Kusine mein Bruder ich meine Schwester mein Vetter meine Kusine

Er ist 1960 geboren.	He was born in 1960.
Ich bin 1982 geboren.	I was born in 1982.
Ich habe am vierten (4.) März Geburtstag.	My birthday is on March 4th.
Mein Geburtstag ist im Januar.	My birthday is in January.
Mein Bruder interessiert sich für Fußball und Briefmarken.	My brother is interested in football and stamps.
Meine Mutter ist Journalistin von Beruf.	My mother is a journalist.
Mein Bruder arbeitet als Maurer.	My brother works as a bricklayer.
Meine Schwester hat eine Stelle bei der Bank/bei Lloyds.	My sister has a job in the bank/at Lloyds.
Ich komme gut mit meiner Schwester aus.	I get on well with my sister.
Ich verstehe mich gut mit meinem Onkel.	I get on well with my uncle.
Meine Eltern sind sehr tolerant.	My parents are very tolerant.
Ich streite mich mit meinem Bruder.	I argue with my brother.

NOTE: Many jobs and occupations are listed in Unit 10.
There is a wider variety of sport and leisure pursuits in Unit 5.

CHECK YOURSELF QUESTIONS

Q1 How would you say this is German?

A I get on well with my grandparents.

B My brothers and I do not get on very well.

C My aunt works at Waitrose/at the supermarket.

D My mother has no brothers or sisters. She is an only child.

E My sister and I are interested in birds.

Q2 You are Charles. Write five sentences introducing your family. Make sure you mention everyone.

Meine Familie

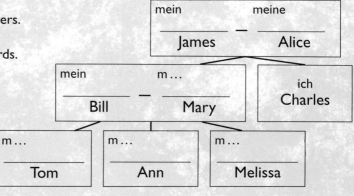

Answers are on page 143.

You could also talk about pocket money or earnings from your part-time job and how you use it.

Ich bekomme fünf Pfund Taschengeld pro Woche/die Woche.	I get five pounds a week pocket money.
Ich arbeite im Supermarkt/im Geschäft am Samstag und ich verdiene…	I work in the supermarket/in the shop on Saturday and I earn…
sehr gut	very good money
zwanzig Pfund pro Tag	£20 a day
drei Pfund pro Stunde	£3 an hour
Ich brauche es für…	I need it for…
Ich spare für…	I am saving for…
Ich gebe es für … aus.	I spend it on…
Platten/CDs/Kassetten	records/CDs/cassettes
Zeitschriften/Comics	magazines/comics
neue Kleidung	new clothes
den Urlaub	my holiday
das Kino	the cinema

? CHECK YOURSELF QUESTIONS

Q1 Tell the examiner that you get no pocket money, but that you work at the supermarket after school for two hours a day. You earn fifty pounds a week and are saving for a motorcycle, but you spend a little every weekend either on a magazine or the cinema.

Answers are on page 144.

☀ Comparison

Comparative of adjectives

■ Regular adjectives form their comparative, as in English, by adding *-er*. In German an umlaut is added to the vowels *a*, *o*, and *u* where possible. The resulting word still needs to agree with its noun as normal.

■ Note the use of *als* to make comparisons:

| *Ich bin größer **als** er.* | I am taller than him. |
| *Er ist älter **als** ich.* | He is older than me. |

The people or things being compared are in the same case, usually the nominative.

Note also the use of *so ... wie* for the English 'as ... as':

| *Er ist **so** groß **wie** sie.* | He is as tall as her. |

Superlative of adjectives

■ Again, this is similar to the English: *-st* or *-est* is added to the adjective. An umlaut is added where possible, as in the comparative.

■ Adjectives ending in *-d, -s, -ß, -sch, -t, -tz* add *-est*.

■ Because they are superlatives (the fastest, the largest, etc.), these words will naturally have the definite article in front of them and take the corresponding adjective endings.

■ Note that these words often become adjectival nouns and are therefore written with a capital letter:

| | *Sie ist die schnellste Läuferin.* | She is the fastest runner. |
| BUT | *Sie ist die Schnellste.* | She is the fastest. |

| | *Das ist das schönste Bild.* | That is the most beautiful picture. |
| BUT | *Das ist das Schönste.* | That is the most beautiful. |

	Adjective	Comparative	Superlative
Regular (-st)	*klein*	*kleiner*	*kleinst-*
	jung	*jünger*	*jüngst-*
	schön	*schöner*	*schönst-*
	schnell	*schneller*	*schnellst-*
	sauber	*sauberer*	*sauberst-*
	wichtig	*wichtiger*	*wichtigst-*
-est	*alt*	*älter*	*ältest-*
	nett	*netter*	*nettest-*
	interessant	*interessanter*	*interessantest-*
Irregular	*gut*	*besser*	*best-*
	groß	*größer*	*größt-*
	hoch	*höher*	*höchst-*
	nah	*näher*	*nächst-*
	viel	*mehr*	*meist-*
			NOTE: *die meisten Leute*

Comparative of adverbs

- The comparative of adverbs is formed in exactly the same way as that of adjectives:

| *Sie läuft schnell.* | She runs fast. |
| *Sie läuft schneller als ich.* | She runs faster than me. |

Superlative of adverbs

- The superlative is also similar, with the addition of *am* and *-en*:
  Er zeichnet am schönsten.

	Adjective	Comparative	Superlative
Regular (-st)	*schön* *schnell*	*schöner* *schneller*	*am schönsten* *am schnellsten*
-est	*schlecht* *oft* *spät*	*schlechter* *öfter* *später*	*am schlechtesten* *am öftesten* *am spätesten*
Irregular	*gern* *gut* *bald* *hoch* *nah* *viel*	*lieber* *besser* *früher* *höher* *näher* *mehr*	*am liebsten* *am besten* *am frühsten* *am höchsten* *am nächsten* *am meisten*

| *Er schreibt besser als ich, aber sie schreibt am schönsten.* | He writes better than I (do), but she writes best of all. |
| *Ich kam später als ich wollte, aber er kam am spätesten.* | I came later than I intended, but he arrived the latest (last) of all. |

? CHECK YOURSELF QUESTIONS

Q1 Complete the following sentences.

A Mein Bruder gewinnt viele Preise im Hochsprung. Er kann _____ springen als alle anderen in seiner Schule.

    hoch   höher   am höchsten

B Mein Freund ist nie pünktlich. Er kommt immer _____ der Lehrer in den Unterricht.

    am spätesten   spät   später als

C Ich trinke gern Kaffee, aber ich trinke manchmal _____ Tee.

D Diese Jacke steht mir nicht; die andere gefällt mir _____.

E Meine Schuhe sind recht dreckig, aber die Schuhe meines Bruders sind noch _____.

Q2 How would you say this in German?

A My eldest brother plays volleyball more often than me.

B Most pupils in the class run faster than me.

C The easiest subject is English.

D I find Technology the hardest.

E My sister finds English (just) as difficult as Technology.

Answers are on page 144.

UNIT 5: FREIZEIT UND FERIEN
LEISURE AND HOLIDAYS

What you need to know

Ich gehe ins Kino/in die Disco/ins Theater.	I go to the cinema/disco/theatre.
Ich gehe zum Jugendklub/zum Stadion.	I go to the youth club/stadium.
Ich spiele gern Fußball/Tischtennis.	I like playing football/table tennis.
Ich treibe gern Sport.	I like doing sport (in general).
Ich gehe gern...	I like going...
angeln	fishing
baden/schwimmen	swimming
joggen	jogging
Ich fahre gern Rad.	I like cycling.
Ich höre gern Musik.	I like listening to music.
Ich höre gern die Popmusiksendungen	I like listening to the pop music
im ersten Programm.	programmes on Radio One.
Ich höre lieber Popmusik als	I prefer listening to pop music
klassische Musik.	than classical music.
Ich spiele Klarinette in einem Orchester.	I play the clarinet in an orchestra.

die Aufführung (en)	performance
die Disco (s)	disco
das Eintrittsgeld (er)	entrance fee/cost
der Fan (s)	fan
der Film (e)	film
der Jugendklub (s)	youth club
die Karte (n)	ticket
die Kasse (n)	box office, cash desk
die Kirmes (sen)	fair
das Kino (s)	cinema
der Klub (s)	club
das Konzert (e)	concert
das Museum (Museen)	museum
das Schauspiel (e)	play
das Schloss (Schlösser)	castle
das Stadion (Stadien)	stadium
das Theater (–)	theater
das Theaterstück (e)	play
die Vorstellung (en)	performance
der Zoo (s)	zoo

MUSIK

die CD (s)	CD
der CD-Player	CD-player
der Kassettenrecorder	cassette recorder
die Platte (n)	record
das Radio	radio
die Stereoanlage	stereo system
das Videogerät (e)	video player

QUESTIONS/PROMPTS

Was machst du am Wochenende?
Spielst du ein Instrument?
Wieviel Taschengeld
   bekommst du?
Was machst du mit dem
   Taschengeld?
Wann/Wohin fährst du in Urlaub?

SPORT

Ich gehe gern spazieren.
Ich reite gern.
Ich segle gern.
Ich laufe gern.
Ich tauche gern.
Ich fahre gern Ski.
Ich wandere gern.
Ich trainiere gern.

Geige

Blockflöte

Klavier

Trompete

Gitarre

Schlagzeug

Flöte

der Computer	computer
das Hobby (s)	hobby
das Interesse (n)	interest
die Karten (*pl*)	cards
das Magazin	magazine
der Roman (e)	novel
die Sammlung (en)	collection
das Taschenbuch (–bücher)	paperback
die Zeitschrift (en)	magazine
basteln	to make things/make models
fotografieren	to take photographs
malen	to paint
zeichnen	to draw

Ich bekomme 5 Pfund pro Woche.	I get £5 a week.
Ich spare für…	I am saving for…
Ich gebe das Geld für … aus.	I spend the money on…
Ich brauche das Geld für…	I need the money for…

Ich fahre … in Urlaub.	I go away on holiday…
in den Osterferien/zu Ostern	in the Easter holidays/at Easter
in den Pfingstferien	in the Whitsun holidays
in den Sommerferien/im Sommer	in the summer holidays/in summer
Wir (Meine Familie und ich) fahren meistens…	We (My family and I) usually go…
an die Küste	to the coast
ans Meer	to the sea
in die Berge	to the hills/mountains
nach Schottland/Wales/Irland	to Scotland/Wales/Ireland

auspacken	to unpack
bleiben	to stay
einpacken	to pack
fahren	to travel
organisieren	to organise
planen	to plan
verbringen	to spend (time)
vorhaben	to plan, intend
zelten	to camp (in a tent)

CHECK YOURSELF QUESTIONS

Q1 Answer the questions in German.

A Was machst du abends?
B Wie oft gehst du ins Kino?
C Wann triffst du dich mit deinen Freunden?
D Was für Sport treibst du?
E Was liest du gern?

Q2 Answer the questions in German.

A Was gibt es für Jugendliche in der Stadt?
B Wo ist das nächste Hallenbad?
C Was kostet der Eintritt im Theater?
D Was für ein Instrument spielst du?
E Wo arbeitest du?

Answers are on page 144.

In the Higher Level Speaking and Writing Tests, you need to be able to talk about your holidays in greater depth. Here are the key questions you should be able to answer:

1	Wann?	When?
2	Wo? Wohin?	Where? Where to?
3	Wie?	How?
4	Mit wem?	With whom?
5	Wo gewohnt?	Stayed where?
6	Das Wetter?	The weather?
7	Was gemacht?	Did what?
8	Gut/nicht gut?	Was it good/not so good?

You can answer each question simply, then follow that basic sentence with another sentence or clause to give a little more detail. For example, here are two different sets of answers to the questions above:

1+2+4 In den letzten Sommerferien war ich mit meiner Familie in Nordwales. Das ist das zweite Mal, dass wir nach Wales gefahren sind.

3 Wir sind mit dem Auto dahin gefahren, aber es war ziemlich viel Urlaubsverkehr auf der Straße, und die Fahrt hat sehr lange gedauert.

5 Wir haben in einer Pension an der Küste gewohnt. Es war nicht sehr teuer, aber auch nicht besonders bequem.

6+7 Das Wetter war einigermaßen gut, und wir haben viele Ausflüge in die Berge gemacht. Wir haben auch einige Museen besucht.

8 Meine Eltern fanden es schön, aber ich fand es ziemlich langweilig. Die Landschaft dort ist ganz herrlich, vor allem die Küste und die Strände waren ganz toll.

1+2 Letztes Ostern bin ich (für) vierzehn Tage mit meinen Freunden nach Frankreich gefahren.

3+4 Wir waren zwei Mädchen und zwei Jungen und sind mit dem Zug und mit der Fähre gereist.

5 Wir haben in einer Jugendherberge gewohnt. Es war extrem billig dort, aber ganz nett und sauber. Die Herbergseltern waren auch ziemlich freundlich. Die Jugendherberge war in einem alten Schloss.

8 Es hat uns dort sehr gut gefallen, und das Essen war prima.

6 Wir hatten herrliches Wetter, und wir haben die meisten Tage am Strand verbracht.

7 Die Stadt um das Schloss war sehr interessant, und wir sind jeden Tag zum Marktplatz gelaufen, um zu sehen, was dort los war.

CHECK YOURSELF QUESTIONS

Q1 1+2+4 Give an account of your last Easter holidays. Say you went with friends to Scotland. It was the first time you had been there.

3 You went by train, but you found the journey very long.

5 You stayed in a youth hostel in a village. It was very cheap but the beds were uncomfortable.

6+7 The weather was fine for the whole week and you went on a trip to the coast. You also visited a castle and a car museum.

8 Your friends found the castle wonderful but you found the museum more interesting. Say you find the countryside great in Scotland.

Answers are on page 145.

How the grammar works

☼ Cases

- The definite and indefinite article alter their form according to their function in the sentence. When you learn the gender of a new word, you are given the nominative case *der*, *die*, *das* of the definite article 'the'. The following table shows how the article changes according to its function in the sentence.

	Masculine	Feminine	Neuter	Plural
Nominative (subject)	*der* *ein*	*die* *eine*	*das* *ein*	*die* –
Accusative (direct object)	*den* *einen*	*die* *eine*	*das* *ein*	*die* –
Genitive ('of')	*des* *eines*	*der* *einer*	*des* *eines*	*der* –
Dative ('to'/'for')	*dem* *einem*	*der* *einer*	*dem* *einem*	*den* –

Nominative

- The nominative is used for the subject of the verb:
  - *Der Wagen fährt schnell.*   *Ein Wagen ist teuer.*
  - *Die Straßenbahn kommt gleich.*   *Eine Straßenbahn erscheint.*
  - *Das Flugzeug landet gleich.*   *Ein Flugzeug ist schneller.*
  - *Die Theaterkarten sind teuer.* (plural)

Accusative

- The accusative is used for the direct object of the verb:
  - *Ich brauche den Kuli.*   *Sie sucht einen Lehrer.*
  - *Ich nehme die Tasche.*   *Ich kaufe eine Theaterkarte.*
  - *Wir essen das Brot.*   *Sie kaufen ein Auto.*

Genitive

- The genitive denotes possession, and is used where we frequently use an apostrophe in English:
  - *Die Farbe des Wagens ist grün.*   The colour of the car is green.
  - *Der Wagen der Krankenschwester ist neu.*   The nurse's car is new.
  - *Die Bilder des Hauses sind alt.*   The pictures of the house are old.
  - *Die Jacken der Kinder sind dreckig geworden.*   The children's jackets got dirty.

Dative

- The dative expresses the idea of 'to' or 'for' in English.
  - *Ich gab dem Lehrer meine Hausaufgaben.*   I gave my homework to the teacher. (I gave the teacher my homework.)
  - *Wir kauften der Frau einen Blumenstrauß.*   We bought a bouquet for the lady.
  - *Ich schenkte dem Mädchen eine Kassette.*   I gave a cassette to the girl. (I gave the girl a cassette.)

☼ Prepositions

- The definite and indefinite articles alter their form when following prepositions. This table shows which case follows each preposition.

Accusative		Dative		Accusative/Dative		Genitive	
bis	until	*aus*	out of	*an*	at, on	*trotz*	despite
durch	through	*bei*	at (someone's house)	*auf*	on	*während*	during
*entlang**	along	*gegenüber***	opposite	*hinter*	behind	*wegen*	because of
für	for	*mit*	with	*in*	in		
gegen	against	*nach*	after	*neben*	near		
ohne	without	*seit*	since	*über*	over, above		
um	around	*von*	from	*unter*	under, below		
		zu	to	*zwischen*	between		

* usually follows the noun   ** sometimes follows the noun

Accusative:	*Ich spiele Volleyball **für eine** Mannschaft.*
Dative:	*Die Katze springt **aus dem** Fenster.*
Genitive:	***Während der** Kunststunde bleiben wir ruhig.*

- The prepositions in the third column take either the accusative or the dative according to their meaning. With the dative they answer the question *wo?* and tell you where someone or something is. With the accusative they answer the question *wohin?* and tell you where someone or something is moving to.

- Here are some of the most common verbs which imply movement or no movement. They should act as a trigger for you when you write a preposition after them.

Accusative:	*gehen, fahren, fallen, fliegen, kommen, reisen, sich setzen, springen, treten*
Dative:	*sich befinden, bleiben, liegen, sein, sitzen*
Accusative for movement:	*Wir **gehen in den** Park.*
	*Der Hund **springt auf das** Sofa.*
Dative for position:	*Wir **sitzen in dem** Park.*
	*Der Hund **liegt auf dem** Sofa.*

❓ CHECK YOURSELF QUESTIONS

Q1 Answer the questions with the prepositions indicated.

A Wie kommst du zur Schule?
  mit   (Say 'by bike'.)
B Wohin gehst du?
  zu   (Say 'to the market'.)
C Für wen kaufst du das?
  für   (Say 'for my friend'.)
D Wo ist der Park?
  gegenüber   (Say 'opposite the bank'.)
E Wohin fährst du?
  in   (Say 'into town'.)

Q2 Complete the sentences with the correct phrase.

A Der Hund jagt die Katze _____
   um das Haus/um dem Haus
B Wir treffen uns _____
   ins Theater/im Theater
C Wir bringen die Teller _____
   ins Esszimmer/im Esszimmer
D Wir kommen _____
   von die Schule/von der Schule
E Die Vase fällt _____
   aus das Fenster/aus dem Fenster

Answers are on page 145.

REVISION SESSION I

▬ What you need to know ▬

Leute treffen, Freunde vorstellen, Abschied nehmen

Grüß Gott!
Servus!
Tschüss!
Darf ich … vorstellen?
Das ist…
Es freut mich (Sie kennen zu lernen)!
Gute Fahrt!
Gute Heimfahrt!
Guten Appetit!
Schlaf gut!
Komm' gut nach Hause!

Meeting people, introducing friends and saying goodbye

Hello! (regional)
Hello! (regional)
Bye!
May I introduce…?
This is…
I'm pleased/A pleasure (to meet you).
Have a good journey!
Have a good journey home!
Enjoy your meal!
Sleep well!
Get home safely!

Pläne machen

Wollen wir ins Kino/Schwimmbad?
Wann treffen wir uns?
Wann wollen wir uns treffen?
Es ist mir egal.
Es macht nichts.
Bis dann.
Bis gleich.
Bis morgen.
Bis nachher.
Bis später.

Making arrangements to meet

Shall we go to the cinema/pool?
When shall we meet?
When shall we meet?
I don't mind./It's all right by me.
It doesn't matter.
See you then.
See you soon.
See you tomorrow.
See you later.
See you later.

---

am Montag	on Monday
montags	on Mondays/every Monday
den ganzen Tag	the whole day
eine halbe Stunde	(for) half an hour
Endlich!	At last!
heute	today
heute vormittag/morgen	this morning
heute nachmittag	this afternoon
im Mai/Juni	in May/June
jeden Tag	every day
jede Woche	every week
morgen (früh)	tomorrow (morning)

WÜNSCHE

Herzlichen Glückwunsch!	Congratulations!
Prost!	Cheers!
Zum Wohl!	Cheers!
Viel Glück!	Good luck!
Viel Spaß!	Have fun!
Entschuldigung!	Excuse me! (Sorry!)
Hoffentlich!	I hope so
Klasse!	Great!
Alles Gute zum Geburtstag!	Happy Birthday!
Frohe Ostern!	Happy Easter!
Frohe/Fröhliche Weihnachten!	Happy Christmas!
Ein frohes/ glückliches neues Jahr!	Happy New Year!

QUESTIONS/PROMPTS

Wann gehst du meistens mit Freunden aus?
Wann fährst du?
Wie lange bleibst du?
Wie lange dauert das?
Wann kommst du wieder?

Q1 Write down the odd one out.

A Guten Tag! Servus! Tschüss!
Grüß Gott!

B Prost! Gute Reise! Guten Appetit!
Zum Wohl!

C Viel Spaß! Quatsch! Viel Glück!
Schönen Abend!

D am Montag morgen früh gestern
heute abend

E Prima! Toll! Schade! Klasse!

Q2 Complete the following dialogue with suitable expressions.

Anton: _____

Bodo: Hallo Anton!

Anton: _____

Bodo: Ganz gut, danke. Und dir?

Anton: _____

Bodo: Darf ich meinen Vetter Hans vorstellen?

Anton: _____?

Hans: Ich komme aus Dresden. Ich bin schon seit einer Woche hier.

Anton: Wann wollen wir ins Kino gehen?

Bodo: _____

Anton: Dann sagen wir Montag gegen acht Uhr.

Bodo: OK. _____
Tschüss!

Answers are on page 146.

Higher vocabulary

Vorschläge

Wie wäre es mit einem Fußballspiel?
Wollen wir nicht lieber ins Kino?

Ich habe (keine) Lust, in die
    Stadt zu gehen.
Hast du Lust dazu?

Suggesting meetings

How about a game of football?
Why don't we go to the cinema?
    (alternative suggestion)
I (don't) fancy going into town.

Do you feel like it?

Schwierigkeiten

Ich verstehe nicht.
Ich habe das nicht verstanden.
Ich weiß nicht.
Könnten Sie das buchstabieren, bitte?
Noch 'mal, bitte.
Was bedeutet das (auf englisch)?
Könnten Sie bitte langsamer sprechen?
Wie sagt man ... auf deutsch?

Handling difficulties

I don't understand.
I didn't understand that.
I don't know.
Could you spell that, please?
Could you repeat that, please?
What does that mean (in English)?
Could you speak more slowly, please?
How do you say ... in German?

CHECK YOURSELF QUESTIONS

Q1 How would you say this in German?

A How about a game of tennis? Do you
fancy playing tennis?
B Wouldn't you rather go to the beach?
C I don't fancy going to the swimming
pool.

D Could you spell your surname, please?
E Excuse me; I didn't understand your
question.

Answers are on page 146.

How the grammar works

☼ Conjunctions

- Conjunctions are words which join main clauses together. There are two kinds: coordinating and subordinating.

- Coordinating conjunctions are easy to use because they don't affect the word order and the verb remains the second idea in the clause. The following words are examples of coordinating conjunctions:

und	and	*aber*	but
denn	for, because	*sondern*	but rather (used to make
oder	or		a contrasting statement)

*Ich nahm meine Kusine mit **und** ich stellte sie meinem Lehrer vor.*
*Sie fand die Englischstunde nicht interessant, **sondern** langweilte sich.*
*Wir konnten nicht in die Stadt fahren, **denn** wir hatten kein Geld.*

- Subordinating conjunctions join a main clause to a subordinate clause, i.e. the clause after the conjunction. The word order in the subordinate clause is altered and the finite verb goes to the end of the clause. Examples of subordinating conjunctions are:

als	when	*obgleich/*	although
bevor	before	*obwohl*	
bis	until	*während*	while
dass	that	*weil*	because
nachdem	after	*wenn*	if, when

HIGHER

damit	so that, in order that
ob	whether
sobald	as soon as
so dass	with the result that

*Sie kann nicht kommen, **weil** sie sich das Bein gebrochen **hat**.*
*Er bleibt heute zu Hause, **damit** er sein Rad reparieren **kann**.*
*Ich weiß nicht, **ob** ich morgen so früh **aufstehe**.**

*Notice how the separable verb and its prefix join up at the end of the clause.

- Your work will be even more impressive if you can master the art of beginning a sentence with the subordinate clause. Look closely at the word order:

***Weil** sie sich das Bein gebrochen **hat, kann** sie nicht kommen.*
***Ob** ich morgen so früh **aufstehe, weiß** ich nicht.*

The word order in the subordinate clause is as before, but the subject and verb in the main clause turn round. This is called inversion, and it brings the two finite verbs together in the middle of the sentence, separated only by a comma. So, if you begin with a subordinating conjunction, remember:

VERB COMMA VERB in the middle of the sentence.

CHECK YOURSELF QUESTIONS

Q1 Add a suitable conjunction to these sentences.

A Er geht heute nicht ins Kino, _____ er kein Geld hat.

B Sie blieben im Geschäft, _____ der Regen endlich aufhörte.

C Sie kommt schnell nach Hause, _____ sie *EastEnders* sehen kann.

D Wir dürfen ausgehen, _____ Mutti nach Hause kommt.

E Ich kann die neue Platte kaufen, _____ ich mein Taschengeld bekomme.

Q2 Complete the following sentences by using a clause from the list below. You will not need to use all of the clauses.

A Weil es stark regnet, …

B Sobald meine Freundin vorbeikommt, …

C Peter besucht morgen seine Großeltern, …

D Ich bleibe morgen mit meinem Bruder zu Hause, …

E Meine Eltern kommen uns abholen, …

1 … weil sie kein Geld hat.

2 … denn meine Mutter muss arbeiten.

3 … ist es sehr sonnig.

4 … obwohl er zu Fuß gehen muss.

5 … gehen wir auf keinem Fall spazieren.

6 … nachdem sie von der Stadt zurückkommen.

7 … können wir zusammen schwimmen gehen.

Answers are on page 147.

UNIT 7: DIE STADT, DIE UMGEBUNG, DAS WETTER

HOME TOWN, LOCAL ENVIRONMENT AND WEATHER

REVISION SESSION 1

▬ What you need to know ▬

QUESTIONS/PROMPTS

Wo wohnst du?
Wo liegt das?
Wie war das Wetter am
  Wochenende?

Ich wohne...	I live...
in Newbury	in Newbury
in einem Dorf	in a village
in einer Stadt	in a town
in einer Großstadt	in a city
in einer Siedlung	on an estate
auf dem Lande	in the country

Newtown liegt...	Newtown is...
im Norden/Süden/Osten/Westen	in the north/south/east/west
in Nordengland/Südengland	in the north/south of England
nicht weit von London	not far from London
in der Nähe von Birmingham	near Birmingham
an der (Süd)küste	on the (south) coast
in den Bergen	in the hills
an der Themse	on the Thames (but *am* for all other rivers: *am Trent*)

Die Stadt/Das Dorf ist...	The town/village is...
relativ klein	relatively small
ziemlich groß	quite large
etwas ruhig	rather quiet
sauber/schmutzig	clean/dirty
angenehm	pleasant

Das Wetter ist herrlich/toll/prima.	The weather is fine/great/marvellous.
Das Wetter ist furchtbar/schrecklich.	The weather is terrible/dreadful.
Es ist heiter.	It's bright.
Es ist regnerisch.	It's rainy.
Es ist trocken.	It's dry.
Es ist nass.	It's wet.
Der Wind kommt aus dem Süden.	The wind is from the south/southerly.

DIE WETTERVORHERSAGE

die Aufheiterung (en)	brighter period	das Hochdruckgebiet	high pressure system
das Gewitter	thunderstorm	das Tiefdruckgebiet	low pressure system
20 Grad Celsius	20 degrees centigrade	die Höchsttemperatur (en)	highest temperature
der Hagel	hail	die Tiefsttemperatur (en)	lowest temperature
der Niederschlag (äge)	rainfall, precipitation	der Schauer (-)	shower
der Wetterbericht (e)	weather report	die Kälte	(the) cold
die Hitze	heat	niederschlagsfrei	dry, i.e. no rain or showers
zeitweise	from time to time	zunehmend	increasing(ly)

DAS WETTER

Es ist sonnig.

Es ist neblig.

Es regnet.

Es friert.

Es ist bewölkt/wolkig.

Es ist stürmisch.

Es schneit.

kalt/kühl/warm/heiß

? CHECK YOURSELF QUESTIONS

Q1 How would you say this in German?

A I live in a large town in the north-east.
B It's a bit dirty, but quite pleasant.
C There is always lots to do.
D The village is quite a long way from the nearest town.
E There's a lot to see in the vicinity.

Q2 How would you say this in German?

A Tomorrow (it) will be cold and cloudy.
B The weather is bright, if somewhat cool.
C There's a northerly wind and it's freezing.
D It's quite wet and rather foggy.
E The lowest temperatures will be around 5 degrees.

Answers are on page 147.

QUESTIONS/PROMPTS

Wie findest du deine Stadt?
Warum?
Was findest du gut daran, und
    was nicht so gut?
Was möchtest du ändern?

Ich wohne sehr gern in Ledbury, weil die Landschaft in der Umgebung so schön ist.	I like living in Ledbury, because the countryside around is so beautiful.
Es gibt schöne Wanderwege am Fluss entlang.	There are nice walks along the river.
Man kann im Wald spazieren gehen.	You can go for walks in the woods.
Das Dorf hat weder Kino/Theater noch Disco/Sportzentrum.	The village has neither cinema/theatre nor a disco/sports centre.
Ich finde den Jugendklub auch nicht so gut, aber man kann mit der Bahn/mit dem Bus in die nächste Stadt fahren.	I don't think much of the youth club either, but you can catch a train/bus to the next town.
Dort gibt es sehr viel zu tun/einen tollen Jugendklub/eine tolle Disco.	There is plenty to do/a great youth club/a fantastic disco there.
Der größte Nachteil ist, dass ich meine Freunde in der Stadt nicht so schnell besuchen kann.	The biggest disadvantage is that I can't visit my friends in town so easily.
Man sollte hier ein Sportzentrum bauen.	They ought to build a sports centre here.
Man könnte hier ein Schwimmbad bauen.	They could build a swimming pool here.
Wir sollten bessere Bus-/Bahnverbindungen haben.	We ought to have a better bus/train service.

CHECK YOURSELF QUESTIONS

Q1 How would you say this in German?

A I like living in Keld, because the countryside around is so beautiful.

B You can go for nice walks in the area.

C The village has neither a disco nor a youth club.

D You can catch a bus to the next town, but I don't think much of the disco there.

E They ought to build a sports centre there.

Answers are on page 148.

☼ Adverbs and adverb phrases

■ An adverb or adverb phrase usually comes as close as possible to the verb which it qualifies, whether the verb is finite:

> *Er spricht langsam.*
> *Kommen Sie schnell her!*

or in the infinitive form:

> *Ich sollte meine Hausaufgaben heute machen.*
> *Mein Vater kann erst morgen kommen.*

☼ Time, Manner, Place

■ Most adverbs and adverb phrases can be put into three main groups: those which describe **when** something happens, those which describe **how** it happens, and those which show **where** it takes place.

■ When you use more than one adverb together in the sentence, you should write them in the order **Time, Manner, Place**:

> *Ich fahre morgen mit dem Rad in die Stadt.*
> *Wir kommen heute abend mit dem Zug in Düsseldorf an.*

■ For emphasis, you can put one adverb at the beginning of the sentence:

> *Morgen fahre ich mit dem Rad in die Schule.*

Notice that the subject and verb are inverted when the adverb comes first in the sentence.

■ The following table shows some more adverbs and phrases which you can use to enhance your writing power, especially at Higher Level.

Time	Manner	Place
gestern	*mit dem Bus*	*in die/der Stadt* *
gestern vormittag/nachmittag/abend	*mit der Bahn*	*in die/der Schule* *
heute	*mit dem Wagen/Auto*	*zur Schule*
heute morgen/nachmittag/abend	*zu Fuß*	*in den/dem Park* *
morgen	*sehr schnell*	*zum Museum*
morgen früh	*langsam*	*ins Kino*
morgen vormittag/nachmittag/abend	*leise*	*die Straße entlang*
um vier Uhr	*laut*	*über die Brücke*
zu Mittag	*plötzlich*	
nach einer Weile/einer halben Stunde		
den ganzen Tag/Abend		

* Look back to Unit 5 for notes on place and movement.

☼ Hin/her

■ These small words are usually found attached to verbs and simply tell you whether the movement of the verb is away from, or towards the speaker. They often correspond to the English 'there' and 'here':

Gehen Sie hin!	Go there.
Kommen Sie her!	Come here.

■ They are very frequently attached to other separable prefixes:

> Geh' **hinunter** in die Küche, hole deine Tasche und komm' wieder **herauf.**

> Geh' **hinauf,** hole deine Sachen und komm' sofort wieder **herunter!**

? CHECK YOURSELF QUESTIONS

Q1 Pick out the adverbs and adverb phrases in this passage and put them in the correct column of the table.

Ich bin gestern mit meiner Mutter in die Stadt gefahren. Wir sind um 8 Uhr losgefahren, denn früh am morgen gibt es viel Verkehr auf der Hauptstraße. Wir haben den Wagen hinter dem Rathaus geparkt, und sind dann zu Fuß zum Markt gelaufen, wo man Obst und Gemüse relativ billig kaufen kann. Gegen 1 Uhr sind wir mit vollen Taschen zum Auto zurückgelaufen.

Time	Manner	Place

Q2 Add at least two adverbs or adverb phrases to each of these sentences.

A Ich habe die Jacke gekauft.
B Wir sind gereist.
C Bringen Sie das Buch!
D Sie kommt mit.
E Wir können nicht fahren.

Answers are on page 148.

UNIT 8: EINKAUFEN
SHOPPING

REVISION SESSION 1 — What you need to know

There are two main areas of shopping vocabulary which you should know. The first is food and drink, much of which was dealt with in Unit 3. The second is clothing. You should also think of a few simple ideas for presents and souvenirs in case you are asked to buy either of these in a role-play.

Ich möchte/Ich hätte gern...	I would like...
ein Kilo Äpfel	a kilo of apples
ein Pfund Birnen	500 grammes (continental pound) of pears
ein halbes Kilo Bananen	half a kilo (500g) of bananas
200 Gramm Wurst	200 grammes of sausage
fünf Scheiben Schinken	five slices of ham
ein Stück Käse	a piece of cheese
eine Schachtel Pralinen	a box of chocolates
ein Paket Waschpulver	a packet of washing powder
ein Päckchen Kaffee	a small packet of coffee
eine Tube Zahnpasta	a tube of toothpaste
eine Tafel Schokolade	a bar of chocolate
eine Flasche Mineralwasser	a bottle of mineral water
eine Dose Limonade	a can of lemonade
eine Tüte	a bag
eine Tragetasche/Plastiktüte	a carrier bag
ein bisschen/etwas	a little/a bit
mehr/weniger	more/less
genug	enough
Ist gut so.	That'll do.
Stimmt so.	That's fine.

die Sandale (n)	sandal
der Schuh (e)	shoe
der Stiefel (-)	boot
der Pantoffel (n)	slipper
der Sportschuh (e)	trainer

aus...	made of...
Baumwolle/Kunststoff	cotton/man-made fibre
Leder/Wildleder	leather/suede
Wolle	wool

die Größe	size
eine Nummer größer/kleiner	a size bigger/smaller

Was darf es sein, bitte?	What would you like?
Werden Sie schon bedient?	Are you being served?
Welche Größe haben Sie?	What size are you?
Sonst noch etwas?	Anything else?
Haben Sie sonst noch einen Wunsch?	Would you like anything else?
Ist das alles?	Is that all?

DIE KLEIDUNG

 die Kleider   clothes   die Kleidung   clothing

 der Anorak (s)

 der Anzug (züge)

 die Badehose (n)

 der Badeanzug (züge)

 die Bluse (n)

 der Gürtel (-)

 der Handschuh (e)

das Hemd (en)

 die Hose (n)

 die Krawatte (n)/der Schlips (e)

 die Jacke (n)

die Jeans (-)

das Kleid (er)

 der Pulli (s)/Pullover (-)

 der Mantel (Mäntel)

 der Rock (Röcke)

 der Schlafanzug (züge)

 die Socke (n)/
der Strumpf (Strümpfe)

 die Strumpfhose (n)

? CHECK YOURSELF QUESTIONS

Q1 The goods and the quantities have got mixed up. Can you correct the sentences?

A Ich möchte eine Tube Schinken.

B Geben Sie mir ein Kilo Waschpulver, bitte.

C Haben Sie ein Paket Äpfel, bitte?

D Und dann hätte ich gern fünf Scheiben Limonade.

E Ich möchte eine Flasche Zahnpasta, bitte.

Q2 How would you say this in German?

A Have you the same (thing) in blue?

B That is too expensive (for me). Have you something cheaper?

C That is too big (for me). Have you a size smaller?

D I'm looking for something for my father.

E Can you wrap it as a present, please?

Answers are on page 149.

Bei der Bank

Nehmen Sie Schecks?
Kann ich mit Kreditkarte bezahlen?
Ich habe nur einen Hunderteuroschein.
Könnten Sie einen Fünfzigeuroschein wechseln?
Wo kann man Geld wechseln?
Ich möchte Reiseschecks wechseln.

Wie steht der Kurs für das Pfund?
Muss ich eine Gebühr bezahlen?
Wo muss ich unterschreiben?
Haben Sie Ihren Ausweis dabei?

At the bank

Do you accept cheques?
Can I pay by credit card?
I only have a 100 euro note.
Have you change for a 50 euro note?
Where can I change some money?
I would like to change some travellers'
    cheques.
What is the exchange rate for the pound?
Do I have to pay a charge?
Where do I sign?
Do you have your passport with you?

Bei der Post

Was kostet eine Postkarte nach England?
Ich möchte dieses Paket nach England schicken.
Wie lange dauert es?
Vier Briefmarken zu 56 Cent, bitte.
Wann ist die nächste Leerung?

At the post office

How much is a postcard to England?
I would like to send this parcel to England.
How long does it take?
Four stamps at 56 cents, please.
When is the next collection?

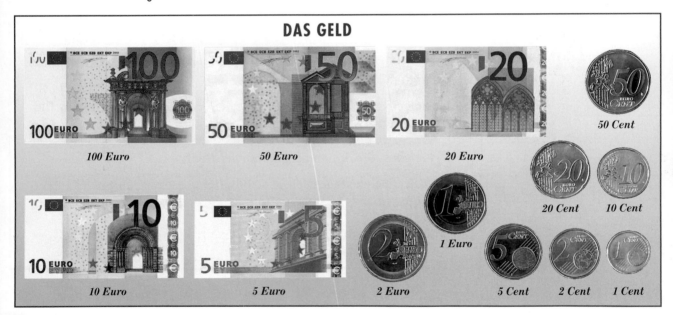

DAS GELD

100 Euro — 50 Euro — 20 Euro — 50 Cent
10 Euro — 5 Euro — 2 Euro — 1 Euro — 5 Cent — 2 Cent — 1 Cent
20 Cent — 10 Cent

? CHECK YOURSELF QUESTIONS

Q1 How would you this say in German?

A Have you change for a 100 euro note, please?

B Can I change money here, please?

C Can my mother pay by credit card?

D What does this parcel cost to England?

E I would like five stamps at €0.51, please.

Answers are on page 149.

■ How the grammar works ■

☼ Adjectives

- Adjectives in German need no agreement when they come after the noun:
    Mein Zimmer ist klein.

    However, they must show their agreement in gender and case when they come immediately before the noun:
    Ich habe ein kleines Zimmer.

- The following chart will give you all the endings you need. You may have seen it as two separate tables for definite and indefinite articles.

Case	Gender			
	Masculine	**Feminine**	**Neuter**	**Plural**
Nominative (subject)	*der* –e *ein* –er	*die* –e *eine* –e	*das* –e *ein* –es	*die* –en –e
Accusative (direct object)	*den* –en *einen* –en	*die* –e *eine* –e	*das* –e *ein* –es	*die* –en –e
Genitive (possessive)	*des* –en *eines* –en	*der* –en *einer* –en	*des* –en *eines* –en	*der* –en –er
Dative ('to'/'for')	*dem* –en *einem* –en	*der* –en *einer* –en	*dem* –en *einem* –en	*den* –en –en

Notice that, below the heavy line, all the adjectives except one (which you are unlikely to use) end in *-en*.

- The adjective endings after *dieser, jener, jeder* and *welcher* follow the same pattern as the endings after the definite article:
    Was ist in diesem kleinen Koffer?
    Welches rote Auto magst du am liebsten?

- The adjective endings after *kein* and after possessive adjectives (*mein, dein*, etc.) follow the same pattern as the endings after the indefinite article:
    Wir haben keine roten Äpfel mehr.
    Unser neues Auto ist grün.

CHECK YOURSELF QUESTIONS

Q1 Complete the adjective endings in this passage.

Mein jünger [1] Bruder lief durch die
offen [2] Tür des groß [3] , weiß [4]
Gebäude [5] und kaufte eine
einfach [6] Fahrkarte nach Bonn.
Mit den beid [7] Koffer [8] in den
Händen ging er den lang [9] Bahnsteig
entlang, bis er den letzt [10] Wagen
erreichte. Peter fand ein leer [11]
Abteil und legte die schwer [12]
Koffer in das altmodisch [13]
Gepäcknetz über dem einzig [14]
freien Platz im ganz [15] Zug.

Q2 Choose the correct words from the box below to complete each sentence.

A Unser VW ist jetzt sehr _____.
Vater möchte einen _____ Wagen
kaufen.

B Ich kaufe mir eine _____ Jacke; die
_____ kann ich nicht mehr
anziehen.

C Der _____ Bus war zu voll, aber
der _____ kommt in fünf Minuten.

D Die Hose ist nicht in der _____
Kommode, sondern im _____
Kleiderschrank.

E Du bist ein _____ Mädchen, aber
mein _____ Fahrrad leihe ich dir
nicht!

> neues   alte   alt   letzte
> neuen   neue   nettes   nächste
> modernen   alten

Answers are on page 149.

UNIT 9: WIE KOMMT MAN DAHIN?
TRAVEL AND TRANSPORT

REVISION SESSION 1

▮ What you need to know ▮

NEHMEN SIE...

die erste	the first on
Straße links	the left
die zweite	the second
Straße links	on the left
die dritte	the third on
Straße rechts	the right
die nächste	the next on
Straße rechts	the right

You need to know how to give and receive directions to places, both on foot and by means of public transport.

Entschuldigen Sie, bitte.	Excuse me, please.
Ich bin hier fremd.	I am a stranger here.
Können Sie mir helfen?	Can you help me?
Wie komme ich...?	How do I get...?
zum Bahnhof/Museum/Rathaus	to the station/museum/town hall
(all masculine and neuter nouns)	
zur Stadtmitte/Post	to the town centre/post office
(all feminine nouns)	
Geht es hier nach Meckenheim?	Is this the way to Meckenheim?
Ist es weit nach/zum/zur...?	Is it far to...?
Wie lange braucht man, um zum Markt zu kommen/laufen?	How long does it take to get/walk to the market place?
Wo ist der Busbahnhof?	Where is the bus station?
Wo ist die nächste Bushaltestelle?	Where is the nearest bus-stop?

Gehen Sie hier geradeaus.	Go straight ahead.
Gehen Sie die Marktstraße entlang.	Go along Market Street.
Gehen Sie die Marktstraße hinunter.	Go down Market Street.
bis an die Ampel/bis ans Rathaus bis zur Ampel/bis zum Rathaus }	as far as the traffic lights/town hall
Biegen Sie links/rechts ab. Biegen Sie nach links/nach rechts. }	Turn left/right.
dem Rathaus gegenüber	opposite the town hall
am Rathaus/an der Galerie vorbei	past the town hall/gallery
Das Rathaus liegt auf der linken Seite.	The town hall is on the left.
Sie können es nicht verfehlen.	You can't miss it.

You should be able to deal with a car breakdown, by saying what is wrong with the vehicle and understanding how to get help.

Gibt es eine Reparaturwerkstatt/eine Tankstelle in der Nähe?	Is there a garage (repairs)/petrol station nearby?
Können Sie unser Auto reparieren?	Can you repair our car?
Wir haben eine Panne.	We've broken down.
Wir haben eine Reifenpanne.	We have a flat tyre.
Der Motor springt nicht an.	The engine won't start.
Wir haben kein Benzin.	We've run out of petrol.
Wir haben ein Problem mit dem Motor/den Bremsen/dem Auspuff.	We have a problem with the engine/brakes/exhaust.
Unsere Windschutzscheibe ist kaputt.	Our windscreen is smashed.
Können Sie einen Mechaniker herausschicken?	Can you send out a mechanic?
Können Sie einen Abschleppwagen schicken?	Can you send out a tow vehicle?
Wie lange dauert es?	How long will it take?

Wir sind auf der Autobahn in der Nähe von Neuß zwischen Düsseldorf und Essen.	We are on the motorway near Neuß between Düsseldorf and Essen.
Wir fahren Richtung Mainz.	We are travelling in the direction of Mainz.
Das Kennzeichen ist…	The registration number is…

An der Tankstelle

At the petrol station

Können Sie das Öl/das Wasser/die Luft nachsehen, bitte?	Can you check the oil/water/air, please?
Ich brauche Öl/Wasser/Luft, bitte.	I need oil/water/air, please.
25 Liter bleifrei/Diesel, bitte.	25 litres of unleaded/diesel, please.

? CHECK YOURSELF QUESTIONS

Q1 How would you say this in German?

A Go past the bridge and take the third on the right.

B Go as far as the lights and turn left.

C The gallery is on the left opposite the town hall.

D Take the next left and carry straight on.

E You can't miss it.

Q2 Complete the dialogue.

Am Telefon

Stimme: Hier Fleischauer.

Sie: Wir haben eine P_____.

Stimme: Was ist denn los?

Sie: Wir haben ein P_____ mit dem M_____. Können Sie einen M_____ s_____?

Stimme: Ja, aber nicht sofort.

Sie: Wie l_____ d_____ es?

Stimme: Eine Stunde. Wo sind Sie?

Sie: Wir sind auf der A_____ in der N_____ von Koblenz. Wir fahren R _____ Bonn.

Answers are on page 150.

ÖFFENTLICHE VERKEHRSMITTEL

mit der U-Bahn

mit der Straßenbahn

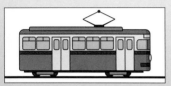

mit der Bahn/dem Zug

mit dem Bus

Here is some language you may hear at the station.

Achtung auf Gleis 8. Der Zug von München fährt gleich ein.	The train from Munich is just arriving at platform 8.
Achtung auf Gleis 10. Der Zug nach Köln fährt gleich ab.	The train standing at platform 10 for Cologne is about to leave.
Bitte einsteigen und Türen schließen!	Please get on and close the doors.
Bitte Achtung beim Einsteigen.	Please take care getting on.
Die Türen schließen automatisch.	The doors close automatically.
Der Zug hat 5 Minuten Verspätung.	The train is five minutes late.

You need to be able to interpret a timetable, finding out such information as types of train, platform number, etc.

gilt nur samstags/sonntags	only valid on Saturdays/Sundays
kein Umtausch	not transferable
mit Zuschlag	with supplement (an extra charge for the faster trains)
Fahrkarten bitte sofort entwerten.	Please stamp your ticket immediately.
verkehrt nur sonntags	only travels on Sundays (found next to an individual train/bus time)

You should be able to report a road accident:

ein Verkehrsunfall	a road traffic accident
der Radfahrer/LKW–Fahrer/Autofahrer	the cyclist/lorry driver/car driver
zu schnell fahren	to drive too fast
zu scharf bremsen	to brake too hard
Er war schuld an dem Unfall.	The accident was his fault.
Niemand war verletzt.	Nobody was hurt/injured.

The single most difficult aspect of reporting an accident is the collision itself, so look at the following examples carefully:

Der Radfahrer ist mit dem Auto zusammengestoßen.	The cyclist collided with the car. (implies they were going towards each other)
Der Lastwagen ist auf das Auto aufgefahren.	The lorry ran into the back of the car.
Das Auto ist gegen einen Baum gefahren.	The car ran into a tree (something stationary)

? CHECK YOURSELF QUESTIONS

Q1 On your preparation card you have a set of pictures which describe an accident. Tell the examiner in your own words what you saw. The gist of the account is set out in the notes below:

- Walking along the road (add a weather phrase for interest), going into town
- Saw a friend cycling towards you, waves and goes past

- Heard a car horn and turned round
- The car collided with the cyclist and then hit a wall
- The cyclist is sitting on the pavement beside the bike, not badly hurt
- You call the police on your mobile phone

Answers are on page 150.

How the grammar works

☼ Pronouns

■ The pronouns you know well are the subject pronouns, which you have learned as part of your verb tables. They are in the nominative case. The table which follows shows these pronouns in the accusative case (direct object) and dative case (indirect object), plus the corresponding pronouns to use with reflexive verbs (see Unit 2).

		Nominative	Accusative	Dative	Reflexive
Singular	I	ich	mich	mir	mich/mir
	you (familiar)	du	dich	dir	dich/dir
	you (formal)	Sie	Sie	Ihnen	sich
	he	er	ihn	ihm	sich
	she	sie	sie	ihr	sich
	it	es	es	ihm	sich
	one	man	einen	einem	sich
Plural	we	wir	uns	uns	uns
	you (familiar)	ihr	euch	euch	euch
	you (formal)	Sie	Sie	Ihnen	sich
	they	sie	sie	ihnen	sich

■ The pronouns are used in exactly the same way as the nouns they are replacing, including after prepositions:

Accusative: *Sie kennen mich.*
Ich besuche ihn.
für ihn
gegen sie
ohne mich

Dative: *Kauf' mir ein Eis, bitte.*
Wie geht's dir?
bei uns
mit Ihnen
zu dir

■ If you need to use the word 'it' after a preposition, you will nearly always need to add the word *da* to the front of the preposition:
Ich schreibe gern mit meinem neuen Kuli. → *Ich schreibe gern damit.*
Ich habe nichts gegen die Idee. → *Ich habe nichts dagegen.*

■ You should learn the rule for the word order of noun and pronoun objects:
  A Two nouns – Dative first:
  Ich gebe dem Mann das Geld.
  B Two pronouns – Accusative first:
  Ich gebe es ihm.
  C Pronoun before noun:
  Ich gebe es dem Mann.
  Ich gebe ihm das Geld.

☀ Relative pronouns: who, whom, whose and which

- The relative pronoun takes its number and gender from the word it refers back to. Its case is determined by the part it plays in the relative clause.

- First, however, you need to be absolutely clear about when to use them. This is not always straightforward, as they are often omitted in English. Look at these two examples. The relative pronoun in each case is in bold:

    The girl, **who** is coming into the room, is my cousin.
    The car, **which** mum bought, was an estate.

    Both these sentences would more likely appear in English as:

    The girl coming into the room is my cousin.
    The car mum bought is an estate.

    In German, the relative pronoun can never be omitted.

- With a few exceptions, the relative pronouns in German are the same as the definite article:

	Masculine	Feminine	Neuter	Plural
Nom./Subject	*der*	*die*	*das*	*die*
Acc./Direct obj.	*den*	*die*	*das*	*die*
Genitive	*dessen*	*deren*	*dessen*	*deren*
Dative/Ind. obj.	*dem*	*der*	*dem*	*denen*

HIGHER

- Relative clauses are subordinate clauses, so the finite verb is the last word in the clause:

    *Der Mann, **der** den Wagen fährt, ist mein Onkel.*
    The man (who is) driving the car is my uncle.

    *Der Mann, **den** ich drüben sehe, ist mein Kunstlehrer.*
    The man (whom) I see over there is my Art teacher.

    *Die Frau, **deren** Auto in der Garage steht, ist unsere Nachbarin.*
    The lady whose car is in the garage is our neighbour.

    *Der Junge, **dem** ich das Buch gab, liest gern Romane.*
    The boy to whom I gave the book enjoys reading novels.

REVISION SESSION 1

■ What you need to know ■

Ich arbeite als Verkäufer(in)* im Supermarkt.
Meine Schwester ist Staatsbeamtin*.
Meine Mutter arbeitet als Busfahrerin*.
Mein Vater hat eine Stelle als Ingenieur*.
Meine Mutter ist Ärztin* von Beruf.

I work as a sales assistant in the supermarket.
My sister is a civil servant.
My mother works as a bus driver.
My father has a job as an engineer.
My mother is a doctor by profession.

*Remember, you do not need the indefinite article *ein/eine* before the job.

BERUFE

Angestellte(r)	employee	Apotheker	chemist	Arbeiter	manual worker
Bauarbeiter	builder	Bauer	farmer	Direktor	director
Drogist	chemist	Elektriker	electrician	Fabrikarbeiter	factory worker
Fahrer	driver	Feuerwehrmann	fireman	Geschäftsmann(frau)	business(wo)man
Krankenpfleger	male nurse	Kaufmann	salesman	Matrose	sailor
Schaffner	(bus) conductor	Soldat	soldier	Schauspieler	actor
Tierarzt	vet	Verkäufer	shop assistant	Zimmermädchen	chamber maid
Zahnarzt	dentist				

NOTE: Job names usually form their feminine by adding *-in*.

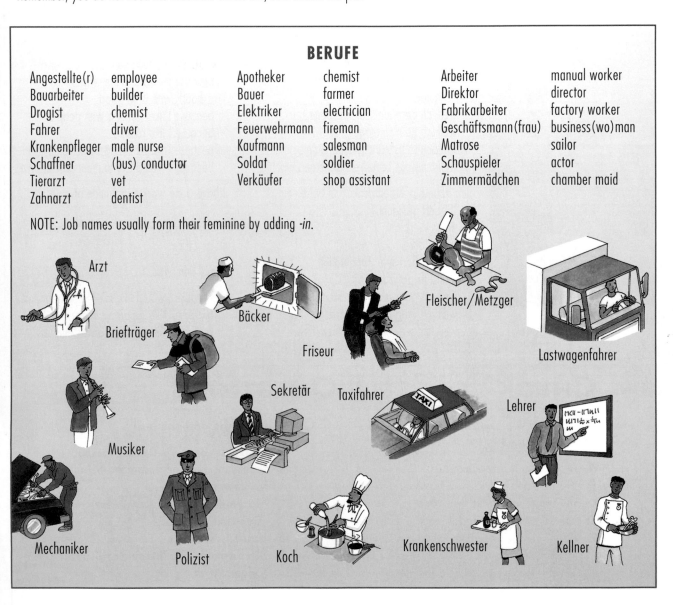

Arzt
Briefträger
Bäcker
Friseur
Fleischer/Metzger
Lastwagenfahrer
Sekretär
Taxifahrer
Lehrer
Musiker
Mechaniker
Polizist
Koch
Krankenschwester
Kellner

Was macht deine Mutter/
dein Vater?
Hast du einen Job?
Arbeitest du am Wochenende?
Hast du ein Arbeitspraktikum
gemacht?

Meine Schwester/Mein Bruder arbeitet...	My sister/brother works...
im Betrieb	in a firm/company
im Büro	in an office
in einer Firma	in a company
im Labor	in a laboratory
in der Industrie	in industry
bei der Bahn	on the railways
mit Computern	with computers
selbstständig	is self-employed
Meine Mutter ist...	My mother is...
arbeitslos	unemployed
berufstätig	employed (i.e. my mother works)
Chef von...	boss of...
angestellt bei...	employed at...

Ich möchte gern ... werden,	I would like to become a ...
weil das Gehalt/der Lohn/der Stundenlohn so gut ist.	because the salary/the wage/the hourly rate is so good.
weil ich gern mit Leuten arbeite.	because I like working with people.
weil ich Routine mag.	because I like routine.
weil ich selbstständig arbeiten möchte.	because I would like to be self-employed.
weil ich neue Leute kennen lernen möchte.	because I would like to meet new people.

Ich trage Zeitungen aus.

Ich habe ein Arbeitspraktikum bei einem Tierarzt gemacht.	I have done work experience at a vet's.
in einer Werkstatt	in a workshop
in einem Büro	in an office
Es hat mir dort sehr gut gefallen, ... } Ich fand es ganz toll, ...	I really enjoyed it...
weil ich gern mit Tieren arbeiten möchte.	because I would like to work with animals.
weil ich Dinge gern repariere.	because I like repairing things.
weil ich gern am Computer arbeite.	because I like working on a computer.

CHECK YOURSELF QUESTIONS

Q1 How would you say this in German? (Use different structures for **A–C**.)

A My father is a mechanic.
B My brother works as a nurse.
C My uncle works at Waitrose.
D My cousin (feminine) is a lorry driver.
E Our neighbour works for herself.

Q2 Which is the odd one out?

A Metzger Bäcker Bauer Friseur
B Lehrerin Kindergärtnerin Schulleiterin Verkäuferin
C Mechaniker Elektriker Bauarbeiter Architekt
D Kinderarzt Arzt Tierarzt Zahnarzt
E Schauspieler Fußballspieler Tänzer Sänger

Answers are on page 151.

Higher vocabulary

Ich gehe/Ich möchte ... gehen,	I am going/I would like to go...
auf die Berufsschule	to further education college
auf die Fachhochschule	to (a technical) university
auf die Universität	to (an academic) university
um Kunst/Mathe/Betriebswirtschaft zu studieren.	(in order) to study Art/Maths/ Business Management.
um einen Kurs/eine Ausbildung in Elektronik zu machen.	(in order) to do a course in Electronics.
Ich mache eine Lehre bei...	I am doing an apprenticeship at...
Ich habe eine Lehrstelle bei...	I have a traineeship with...
Ich bleibe hier an der Schule/in der Oberstufe.	I'm staying on at school/in the sixth form.
Zunächst mache ich meine A-levels in Deutsch, Englisch und Geschichte.	First of all I'm going to do my A-levels in German, English and History.
In zwei Jahren weiß ich besser Bescheid was ich studieren möchte.	I'll know better in two years what I would like to study.

CHECK YOURSELF QUESTIONS

Q1 Give three different options for your education or career path after your GSCE exams.

For example:
• You are going to get a job straight away.
• You are staying on to study at school: say which subjects.
• You are going to a further education college to study a course in...

Answers are on page 152.

■ How the grammar works ■

☼ The future tense

■ Just as in English, you can use the present tense to suggest future intent:

Ich gehe nächstes Jahr auf die Berufsschule.	I am going to college next year.
Ich mache im September eine kaufmännische Ausbildung.	I am taking a business course in September.
Ich arbeite ab ersten August in der Bank.	I am working in the bank from August 1st.

■ However, you should also know how to form the future tense using the present tense of *werden* with an infinitive, in case you are asked a question in that way during your Speaking Test. So, if you are asked:

Was wirst du/werden Sie nächstes Jahr machen?

you could answer:

Ich werde nächstes Jahr auf die Berufsschule gehen.
Ich werde im September eine kaufmännische Ausbildung machen.
Ich werde ab ersten August in der Bank arbeiten.

☼ Using the infinitive

■ You should be able to use the infinitive in the following ways:

1 **After the six modal verbs and *lassen*:**

Darf ich heute abend ins Kino gehen?	(*dürfen*)
May I go to the cinema tonight?	
Ich kann sehr gut schwimmen.	(*können*)
I can swim very well.	
Magst du gern reiten?	(*mögen*)*
Do you like riding?	
Wir müssen unsere Hausaufgaben machen.	(*müssen*)
We must do our homework.	
Ihr sollt bei diesem Wetter nicht in den Park gehen.	(*sollen*)
You shouldn't go to the park in this weather.	
Wir wollen im Sommer nach Schottland fahren.	(*wollen*)
We want (intend) to go to Scotland this summer.	
Ich lasse mir heute die Haare schneiden.	(*lassen*)
I'm having my hair cut today.	

*Most commonly, of course, after *Ich möchte* (I would like).

HIGHER + FOUNDATION UNDERSTANDING

2 **After certain other verbs with *zu*:**

Ich hoffe, am Wochenende Fußball zu spielen.	(*hoffen*)
I hope to play football at the weekend.	
Ich brauche es heute nicht zu machen.	(*brauchen*)
I don't need to do it today.	

3 **After *um ... zu*:**

Ich gehe in die Stadt, um einen neuen Schreibblock zu kaufen.
I'm going into town to buy a new writing pad.

4 After *gehen*:

> *Ich gehe heute in der Stadt einkaufen.*
> I'm going shopping in town today.
> *Wir gehen morgen schwimmen.*
> We're going swimming tomorrow.

☼ Interrogatives

■ You should know at least two of the following ways of forming questions:

1 By inverting (turning round) subject and verb:

> *Gehst du heute zur Schule?*

2 By adding *ja?, nicht?, oder?* or *nicht wahr?* to a statement:

> *Das ist dein Buch, nicht wahr?*
> *Mutti kommt mit, oder?*

3 By introducing the question with an interrogative word:

> *Was machst du?*
> *Wann kommt sie nach Hause?*
> *Wie machen sie das?*
> *Was für Bücher liest du gern?*
> *Wie viele Leute kommen heute abend?*
> *Warum darfst du nicht kommen?*

☼ Negatives

■
kein	no, not one
nichts	nothing
gar nicht/überhaupt nicht	not at all
nie/niemals	never
niemand	no-one, nobody
nirgends/nirgendwo	nowhere

> *Ich habe **kein** Geld bei mir.*　　I have no money on me.
> *Wir haben ihn **nirgends** gesehen.*　We haven't seen him anywhere.
> *Ich mag Pizza **überhaupt nicht**.*　　I don't like pizza at all.
> *Wir haben **niemanden** getroffen.*　We didn't meet anyone.

Note that *jemand* and *niemand* add *-en* in the accusative and dative.

? Check Yourself Questions

Q1 Translate the following into English.

A Mein Bruder studiert Medizin an der Universität.

B Unser Nachbarssohn macht eine Lehre bei Siemens.

C Wann musst du in der Berufsschule anfangen?

D Möchten Sie nicht lieber Tierarzt werden?

E Wie viel wirst du als Lehrling verdienen?

Q2 Complete the questions with the correct form of the modal verb shown in brackets.

A Warum _____ ihr mir nicht helfen? (können)
Why can't you help me?

B Um wie viel Uhr _____ du sie treffen? (müssen)
What time must you meet them?

C Wie viel _____ ich mitnehmen? (dürfen)
How many/much may I take?

D Wann _____ man in Düsseldorf ankommen? (sollen)
When are we supposed to arrive in Düsseldorf?

E _____ ihr nicht mitkommen? (wollen)
Don't you want to come along?

Answers are on page 152.

UNIT 11: AM ARBEITSPLATZ
AT WORK

 **REVISION SESSION I**

■ What you need to know ■

You should be able to take or leave messages at your place of work.

Hier Schmidt.	This is Mr/Ms Smith speaking.
Darf ich ihn/sie sprechen, bitte?	May I speak to him/her, please?
Es tut mir leid.	I'm sorry.
Frau Bergemann ist im Moment geschäftlich unterwegs.	Mrs Bergemann is out on business at present.
Herr Kolbitz ist nicht im Büro/außer Haus.	Mr Kolbitz is not in the office.
Kann/Darf ich ihm/ihr etwas ausrichten?	Can/May I take/give him/her a message?
Könnten Sie ihm/ihr bitte etwas ausrichten?	Could you please give him/her a message?
Ich schreibe ihm/ihr einen Zettel.	I'll write him/her a note.
Ich lege ihm/ihr einen Zettel auf den Tisch.	I'll put a note on his/her desk.
Ich sage/gebe ihm/ihr Bescheid.	I'll give him/her the message.
Er ist jeden Moment wieder da.	He will be back any minute.
Sie ist in einer halben Stunde wieder da.	She will be back in half an hour.

You should be able to understand simple instructions in the workplace.

Lesen Sie die Betriebsanleitung.	Read the instructions for use (machines).
einschalten, ausschalten	switch on, switch off
der Computer/PC/Laptop	computer/PC/lap-top
betriebsbereit	'ready'
drucken/der Drucker (–)	to print/printer
das Memory/der Speicher	memory
der Netzanschluss (schlüsse)	mains (power) connection
der Rechner	calculator
die Software	software
speichern	to save
die Tastatur (en)	keyboard
weiter	continue
das Zeichen (–)	sign, character
der Anrufbeantworter (–)	answering machine
das Handy (s)	mobile phone

You should be able to make arrangements to be contacted, or have information sent by phone, fax or e-mail.

Ich bin unter dieser Nummer/auf meinem Handy zu erreichen.	I can be contacted on this number/on my mobile.
Rufen Sie mich bitte an!	Please call/telephone me.
Bitte schicken Sie ein Fax.	Please send a fax.
Haben Sie ein Modem?	Do you have you a modem?

You should be able to write a letter and fill out simple forms relating to a job application.

Ich bin am 14. Januar 1986 in Reading geboren.	I was born in Reading on the 14th January 1986.
Ich lerne Deutsch seit fünf Jahren.	I've been learning German for five years.
Ich habe Ihre Anzeige in der Tageszeitung gelesen.	I saw your advertisement in the newspaper
Ich könnte zum 1. September anfangen.	I'm available to start work from 1st September.
Könnten Sie mir bitte weitere Details zuschicken?	Please would you send me further information (about the job)?

ICH SUCHE EINE STELLE!

Betrifft	concerning (at the top of a letter/fax, etc.)	ledig/verheiratet/geschieden	single/married/divorced
		das Geburtsdatum/geboren am ...	date of birth ...
das Angebot (e)	offer	ich füge bei/ich lege bei	I enclose
die Bewerbung	application	das Schulzeugnis	school report
sich bewerben	apply	der Lebenslauf	curriculum vitae (C.V.)
die Staatsangehörigkeit	nationality	der Empfehlungsbrief (e)	reference
der Familienstand	marital status	Ich interessiere mich für ...	I'm interested in ...

CHECK YOURSELF QUESTIONS

Q1 How would you say this in German?

A May I speak to Rudi, please?
B Can you give Mr Braun a message, please?
C I'll tell her immediately.
D Would you prefer to send a fax?
E She'll be back (in the office) around 2.

Q2 Complete the form below.

Bitte in Druckschrift schreiben

Familienname . . . .
Vorname . . . .
geboren am . . . .

Familienstand
ledig/verheiratet/geschieden
(bitte durchstreichen)
Staatsangehörigkeit . . . .

Adresse
Straße . . . .
Ort . . . .
PLZ . . . .

Telefonisch zu erreichen? ja/nein

tagsüber . . . .
abends . . . .

Answers are on page 152.

You should be able to act as an interpreter at work.

Frau White sagt, dass sie erst morgen kommen kann.	Mrs White says that she can't come until tomorrow.
Sie meint, dass der Wagen nicht in Ordnung ist.	She says that the car is not right.
Sie glaubt, dass die Bremsen nicht richtig funktionieren.	She believes that the brakes are not working properly.
Sie hofft, dass wir den Wagen morgen reparieren können.	She hopes that we can repair the car tomorrow.
Sie fragt, wann sie kommen soll.	She is asking when she should come.
Sie fragt, ob wir ihr das Auto zurückbringen können.	She is asking whether we can bring the car back to her.

NOTE: Don't forget to change the word order after *dass* (see Unit 6).

CHECK YOURSELF QUESTIONS

Q1 How would you say this in German?

    A She says she can't come this afternoon.
    B He hopes we can come tomorrow.
    C They are asking what time we will arrive.
    D I have asked him whether the car is OK.
    E He says that we should come as soon as possible.

Answers are on page 153.

▬ How the grammar works ▬

☼ Imperatives _____

■ The imperative of a verb tells you to do something or, in many cases, **not** to do it. You need to recognise certain conventions when giving other people orders, or making polite requests.

■ In a formal situation, use the *Sie* form of the verb as follows:

Nehmen Sie Platz!	Take a seat/Sit down.
Kommen Sie bitte mit!	Please come with me.
Bitte unterschreiben Sie hier!	Please sign here.

Don't be put off by the exclamation mark. It is simply a convention – it doesn't mean that someone is shouting at you.

■ In informal situations, such as with friends and family, a different style of command is used. This is adapted from the *du* form of the verb, by taking off the *-st* ending and adding either an *-e* or an apostrophe:

Komm' mit!	Come with me.
Bringe deine Tasche mit!	Bring your bag with you.
Setz' dich!	Sit down.

■ If you are talking to more than one friend or member of the family, you use the *ihr* form of the imperative, as follows:

Kommt mit!	Come with me.
Bringt eure Taschen mit!	Bring your bags with you.
Setzt euch!	Sit down.

■ You should also recognise the most obvious public notices. In German these simply use the infinitive form:

Bitte Hände waschen.	Wash your hands, please. (in a public toilet)
Nicht hinauslehnen.	Don't lean out. (of the window on trains)
Bitte anklopfen.	Please knock.

? CHECK YOURSELF QUESTIONS

Q1 Your teacher is talking to you individually. What would she say if she wanted you to ...

A ... show her your homework?
B ... sit down?

What would she say to the class if she wanted you to ...

C ... get your books out?
D ... write the date?
E ... carry on?

Q2 Your friend, Tom, phones and asks you to pass on the following message to his penfriend's mother. What do you say to her?

Tom: Tell Frau Marx I can't come home till 8 o'clock. The next bus will arrive at 7.50. Ask her what time the supermarket shuts, and if I should buy anything for her. Tell her I'm very tired.

Answers are on page 153.

REVISION SESSION 1

What you need to know

You should be able to talk about a wide range of experiences abroad, saying what you saw and did.

Wie war die Reise?

Wir sind geflogen.
Der Flug nach Berlin dauerte anderthalb Stunden.
Wir sind mit der Bahn gefahren.
Die Fahrt/Die Reise dauerte sieben Stunden.
Die Überfahrt war sehr ruhig/stürmisch.
Wir mussten in Brüssel umsteigen.
Wir sind um 7 Uhr morgens abgefahren.
Wir sind um 8 Uhr abends angekommen.

How was the journey?

We flew.
The flight to Berlin took one and a half hours.

We travelled by train.
The journey took seven hours.
The ferry crossing was very calm/rough.
We had to change trains in Brussels.
We left at 7 in the morning.
We arrived at 8 in the evening.

Auf dem Campingplatz

Wir haben einen Zeltplatz gefunden.
die Anmeldung
die Gebühr (en)
Wir haben das Zelt aufgebaut/aufgeschlagen.
Wir haben das Zelt abgebaut.
Ich habe die Klappstühle aus dem Auto genommen.
Ich habe den Klapptisch aufgestellt.

At the campsite

We found a place for the tent/a 'pitch'.
reception/office
fees/charges
We put up the tent.
We took down the tent.
I got the folding chairs out of the car.

I put up the folding table.

In der Jugendherberge

der Herbergsvater/die Herbergsmutter
Die Herbergseltern waren sehr freundlich.
Wir haben Schlafsäcke geliehen.
Der Schlafraum (räume) war im ersten Stock.
Es war verboten, nach 10 Uhr laute Musik zu spielen.
Man hat uns erlaubt, den Hausschlüssel mitzunehmen.

At the youth hostel

warden (male and female)
The wardens were very friendly.
We hired sleeping bags.
The dormitory was on the first floor.
It was forbidden to play loud music after 10 o'clock.
We were allowed to take the door key with us.

Im Hotel

Haben Sie ein Zimmer frei?
Ich möchte ein Einzelzimmer, bitte.
Wir bleiben drei Nächte.
Um wie viel Uhr gibt es Frühstück/Abendessen?
Wir haben uns gleich angemeldet.
Wir hatten zwei Zimmer reserviert.
Das Hotel war leider voll.
Die Empfangsdame war sehr hilfsbereit.
Sie hat uns ein anderes Hotel empfohlen.

At the hotel

Do you have a room available?
I'd like a single room.
We shall be staying three nights.
What time is breakfast/dinner?

We checked in straight away.
We had reserved two rooms.
The hotel was unfortunately full.
The receptionist was very helpful.
She recommended us another hotel.

WIE SIND SIE GEFAHREN?

mit der Fähre

mit dem Auto/Wagen

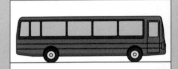

mit dem Reisebus

IM HOTEL

 ein Einzelzimmer

 ein Doppelzimmer

 mit Dusche

 mit Bad

Wir mussten ein Anmeldungsformular ausfüllen.	We had to complete a form at the reception.
Unser Aufenthalt in Bonn dauerte fünf Tage.	Our stay in Bonn lasted five days.
Von unserem Fenster haben wir eine herrliche Aussicht über den Rhein gehabt.	From our window we had a superb view over the Rhine.
Der Aufenthaltsraum war im Erdgeschoss.	The lounge was on the ground floor.
Es gab ab 7 Uhr Frühstück.	Breakfast was served from 7 o'clock onwards.
Wir haben Halbpension/Vollpension gehabt.	We had half board/full board.
Der Preis war inklusiv.	The price was inclusive.
Alle Zimmer hatten fließendes Wasser.	All rooms had running water.
Wir haben uns über den Lärm beschwert/beklagt.	We complained about the noise.

You should be able to ask for details about a town or region you plan to visit, and give similar details about your own area to a prospective tourist.

QUESTIONS/PROMPTS

Wo warst du in den Ferien?
Was hast du in den Ferien gemacht?
Hast du Ausflüge gemacht?

Im Verkehrsamt	In the tourist office
Was gibt es hier in der Nähe zu sehen und zu tun?	What is there to see and do in the area?
Was sollte man hier sehen?	What ought we to see here?
Haben Sie einen Stadtplan, bitte?	Do you have a street map, please?
Können Sie ein preiswertes Hotel in der Nähe/Stadt empfehlen?	Can you recommend a reasonable (cheap) hotel in the area/town?
Haben Sie ein Hotelverzeichnis?	Do you have a list of hotels, please?
Kann man irgendwo Fahrräder leihen?	Can you hire bikes somewhere?
Kann man eine Stadtrundfahrt/einen Stadtrundgang machen?	Can we do a guided tour of the town? (in a bus or on foot)
Ich hätte/möchte gern einen Busfahrplan.	I would like a bus timetable, please.
Wir möchten gern das Schloss besichtigen.	We would like to visit the castle/palace.
Wie kommt man am besten dahin?	What is the best way to get there?

? CHECK YOURSELF QUESTIONS

Q1 Complete the following passage.

Wir s_____ letzt_____
Sommer mit der B_____ nach
Düsseldorf gef_____. Die Reise
da_____ zehn St_____.

Mein Freund und ich ha_____
Schl_____ reserv_____,
weil wir über Nacht gef_____
s_____. Wir m_____ in
Lille um _____. Wir s_____
gegen Mittag in Düsseldorf an
_____.

Q2 Put these sentences into the correct order to make a sensible account.

1 Wir haben gegen sieben Uhr in der Pizzeria zu Abend gegessen.
2 Wir sind auf unsere Zimmer gegangen.
3 Ich bin ins Verkehrsamt gegangen.
4 Ich habe mich geduscht und mich umgezogen.
5 Wir sind zum Hotel gefahren und haben in der Tiefgarage geparkt.
6 Wir sind um vier Uhr nachmittags in Bonn angekommen.
7 Wir haben uns gleich angemeldet.
8 Man hat uns ein preiswertes Hotel empfohlen.

Answers are on page 153.

Higher vocabulary

You should be able to discuss a part of a German-speaking country you know.

Düsseldorf ist eine reizende Stadt.	Düsseldorf is an attractive city.
Die Altstadt ist weltberühmt.	The old part of town is world famous.
Die Stadt hat eine große Messe und liegt am Rhein.	The town has a large trade fair and lies on the Rhine.
Vom Rheinturm hat man eine traumhafte Aussicht in alle Richtungen.	From the Rhine tower there is a magnificent view in all directions.
Es gibt das zauberhafte Schloss Benrath.	There is the wonderful Benrath Palace.

You should be able to compare features of the foreign country with your own area and to express opinions about what you saw and did.

Düsseldorf ist weitaus größer als Newtown.	Düsseldorf is considerably larger than Newtown.
viel schöner als	much more beautiful than
nachts lebendiger als	more lively at night than
ganz anders als	quite different from
Düsseldorf hat mehr große Kaufhäuser als Newtown.	Düsseldorf has more large department stores than Newtown.
ein besseres Verkehrsnetz	a better public transport network
mehr und größere Museen	more and bigger museums
Ich fand die Altstadt ganz toll.	I found the old part of town great.
etwas komisch	somewhat strange
ganz lustig	quite funny
erstaunlich	astonishing
ein bisschen deprimierend	a little depressing
Die Sehenswürdigkeiten waren…	The sights were…
höchst interessant	extremely interesting
teurer als ich ewartet hatte	more expensive than I had expected
noch freundlicher als ich gehofft hatte	even more welcoming than I had hoped

CHECK YOURSELF QUESTIONS

Q1 How would you say this in German?

A The department stores are world famous.

B The old town is livelier than our town.

C The public transport system in town is not as big as here.

D The local sights are much more interesting than [your home town].

E I found the castle very impressive.

Answers are on page 154.

◼ How the grammar works ◼

☀ Verb tenses

The imperfect tense

■ The imperfect tense is used:

- to report events in the past in newspaper and magazine articles
- to record the prevailing weather
- to report people's mood and feelings.

  Es war gestern sehr stürmisch und es regnete fast den ganzen Tag.

You need to **recognise** the imperfect more often than you need to use it.

■ The endings of weak (regular) and strong (irregular) verbs are as follows:

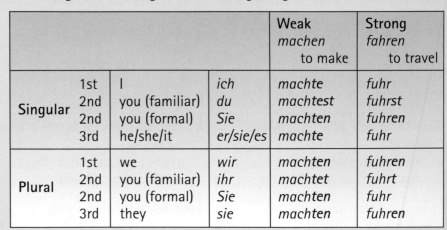

				Weak *machen* to make	Strong *fahren* to travel
Singular	1st	I	ich	machte	fuhr
	2nd	you (familiar)	du	machtest	fuhrst
	2nd	you (formal)	Sie	machten	fuhren
	3rd	he/she/it	er/sie/es	machte	fuhr
Plural	1st	we	wir	machten	fuhren
	2nd	you (familiar)	ihr	machtet	fuhrt
	2nd	you (formal)	Sie	machten	fuhr
	3rd	they	sie	machten	fuhren

However, it is very unlikely that you will ever need the 'you' forms of the imperfect. The remaining endings are extremely easy to remember:

	Weak	Strong
Singular	-te	—
Plural	-ten	-en

The perfect tense

■ You need to be thoroughly confident in your use of the perfect tense to describe events in the past such as:

- what you did last night, or last weekend
- where you went with the school on a trip
- where you went, what you saw and did on holiday.

■ The perfect tense of all verbs is formed by using the auxiliary verb *haben* or *sein* with the past participle of the verb concerned:

  Ich habe gestern Tennis gespielt.
  Wir sind oft schwimmen gegangen.

- You need to know the past participles of at least 50 strong (irregular) verbs from memory. Many strong verbs fall into groups that have the same pattern of vowel change in their different tenses. It is usually a help to learn a group together. For example, try the group like:

biegen	*biegt*	*bog*	*gebogen*
fliegen	*fliegt*	*flog*	*geflogen*

- Regular weak verbs form their past participle using the *ge -t* rule:

  lernen → *gelernt*   *machen* → *gemacht*

  When the stem of the verb ends in *-d* or *-t*, the past participle ends in *-et*:

  arbeiten → *gearbeitet*   *landen* → *gelandet*

- Certain groups of verbs have different ways of forming past participles:

  - All separable verbs add *ge* between the prefix and the rest of the verb:

    Weak separable   **Strong separable**
    einschalten → *eingeschaltet*   *ankommen* → *angekommen*

  - Inseparable verbs do not have the *ge* in their past participle, but simply end with *-t* or *-en* according to whether they are weak or strong. These verbs have the prefixes *be-*, *emp-*, *ent-*, *er-*, *ge-*, *miss-*, *ver-* and *zer-*:

    Weak inseparable   **Strong inseparable**
    bezahlen → *bezahlt*   *empfangen* → *empfangen*
    erzählen → *erzählt*   *entscheiden* → *entschieden*
    verpassen → *verpasst*   *gefallen* → *gefallen*
    zerstören → *zerstört*   *missverstehen* → *missverstanden*

  - Weak verbs ending in *-ieren* need no *ge* to form their past participle:
    kapieren → *kapiert*   *reparieren* → *repariert*

The pluperfect tense

- You need to recognise the pluperfect tense and be able to use one or two examples of it in a narrative, for example, in describing what you **had** done, or what had happened **before** the event you are now describing.

- The pluperfect is formed by adding the imperfect of the auxiliary, *haben* or *sein*, to the past participle of the verb concerned:
  Ich hatte gemacht.
  Ich war angekommen.

- The pluperfect is frequently used after the conjunctions *bevor*, *nachdem*, *weil*, *als*, *sobald*, etc. Remember that you then need to change the word order:
  Wir hatten schon um 6 Uhr gegessen, bevor wir ins Kino gegangen sind.
  Weil das Wetter so schön war, waren wir schon schwimmen gegangen.

HIGHER
+
FOUNDATION UNDERSTANDING

CHECK YOURSELF QUESTIONS

Q1 Put the following verbs under the correct heading in the table below. Then write down the past participle of each one.

Past participle

vorbereiten _____

anfangen _____

überraschen _____

einschlafen _____

aufstehen _____

empfehlen _____

aufräumen _____

verkaufen _____

vorschlagen _____

erzählen _____

Q2 Complete each of the following sentences using the correct version of the phrases in brackets.

A Ich war froh, dass ich…
(mein Portemonnaie finden)

B Mutti schien sehr böse, weil wir…
(sich verlaufen)

C Wir waren zufrieden, als wir…
(die Arbeit zu Ende schreiben)

D Sie waren alle überrascht, nachdem meine Oma…
(die Geschichte erzählen)

Weak		Strong	
Separable	**Inseparable**	**Separable**	**Inseparable**

Answers are on page 154.

All GCSE syllabuses include a section to do with world events and issues. You may meet these in the Reading and Listening Tests, but you are likely to be more comfortable with other topics when it comes to the Speaking and Writing Tests. It is advisable to steer clear of them in the Speaking Test especially, where you could quickly be lost for the necessary vocabulary.

Accordingly, there are fewer exercises in the Check yourself sections. However, the words and phrases below will help you understand at least the outline of an issue in the wider world.

REVISION SESSION 1

What you need to know

Nachrichten und Aktuelles — News and current affairs

die Dritte Welt	the Third World
das Entwicklungsland (länder)	developing country
die Feier (n)	celebration, festivity
das Fest (e)	festival
der Frieden	peace
der Krieg	war
die Katastrophe/katastrophal	catastrophe/catastrophic
die Klimaänderung	climate change
die Armut	poverty
die Hungersnot	famine
das Erdbeben	earthquake
die Überschwemmung (en)	floods
das Hochwasser	floods
das Gewitter	storm
ums Leben kommen	to die, be fatally injured

Grüne Themen — Green issues

die Umwelt	environment
umweltfreundlich	environmentally friendly
bleifreies Benzin	unleaded petrol
der Altglascontainer (–)	bottle bank
die Altkleidersammlung (en)	collection of old clothes
die Wiederverwertung/das Recycling	recycling
die Müllverwertung	waste recycling

Gesundheitsthemen — Health issues

gesund/ungesund	healthy/unhealthy
das Rauchen	smoking
das Rauschgift (e)	drugs
der Alkohol	alcohol
der Vegetarier/in	vegetarian

Was meinen Sie dazu?	What is your opinion?
Ich finde es furchtbar, dass...	I think it is terrible that...
Ich war sehr überrascht zu hören, dass...	I was very surprised to hear that...
Wir waren schockiert, als wir die Nachricht(en) hörten.	We were shocked when we heard the news.
Ich war froh, als ich hörte, dass...	I was pleased when I heard that...
Wir sollten etwas machen.	We ought to do something.
Man muss mehr machen, um das zu vermeiden.	We must do more to avoid that.
Ich halte es für äußerst wichtig, dass...	I think it is extremely important that...
Ich kann es nicht leiden, wenn...	I can't bear it when...

LAND – PERSON – STAATSANGEHÖRIGKEIT

England
Engländer/in –
englisch

Schottland
Schotte/in –
schottisch

Wales
Waliser/in –
walisisch

Irland
Ire/Irin – irisch

Belgien
Belgier/in –
belgisch

Frankreich
Franzose/ösin –
französisch

Griechenland
Grieche/in –
griechisch

Holland/die
Niederlande
Holländer/in –
holländisch

Deutschland
Deutscher/
Deutsche –
deutsch

Italien
Italiener/in –
italienisch

Österreich
Österreicher/in –
österreichisch

Spanien
Spanier/in –
spanisch

Amerika/die
Vereinigten
Staaten
Amerikaner/in –
amerikanisch

Schweiz
Schweizer/in –
schweizerisch

die Türkei
Türke/in –
türkisch

? CHECK YOURSELF QUESTIONS

Q1 How would you say this in German?

A In my opinion, smoking is unhealthy.
B We were all shocked by the news about an earthquake in Turkey.
C There seems no end to the famine in Africa.
D We must do more to protect the environment.

Answers are on page 155.

☀ Pronouns

Indefinite pronouns

■ You should be able to **use** the following indefinite pronouns:

Jeder kann das machen.	Everyone can do it.
Ein paar sind ausgefallen.	A few dropped out.
Einige sind verhungert.	Some starved.
Andere haben den Weg verloren.	Others lost their way.

■ You should be able to **recognise** the following indefinite pronouns:

Jemand hat das vorgeschlagen.	Someone suggested it.
Ich habe niemanden* gefunden.	I found no-one.
Mehrere sind zurückgeblieben.	Some stayed behind.
Manche wollten nicht mitfahren.	Some did not want to go.
Man konnte nur wenig machen.	We could do only little.

*Used here in the accusative.

Interrogative pronouns

■ You should be able to use these **interrogative pronouns**:

Wer hat das behauptet?	Who said that?
Wen haben Sie dort gesehen?	Who/Whom did you see there?
Wessen ist das?	Whose is it?
Welcher kommt zuerst?	Which comes first?

Demonstrative pronouns

■ You should be able to use these **demonstrative pronouns**:

Ich mag diesen nicht.	I don't like the latter (this one). (Accusative)
Jener ist viel besser.	The former (that one) is much better. (Nominative)

HIGHER
+
FOUNDATION UNDERSTANDING

 CHECK YOURSELF QUESTIONS

Q1 How would you say this in German?

A Some are happy about it; others are not content.

B A few have left, but nobody saw them.

C There is only little one can do.

D Everyone should do something, but nobody wants to.

E Which arrived today, this one or that one?

Answers are on page 155.

REVISION SESSION 1

How to overcome problems

☀ Problems and solutions

There are some specific difficulties associated with listening. This unit will help you to identify ways in which you can improve your comprehension of spoken German so that you improve your performance in your exam.

Problem 1

Your concentration on the two hearings of the recording is vital. You can't ask for it to be played again (unlike in the Reading Test where you can look at the passages as much as you like within the time allowed.)

Solution

Practise concentrating on something recorded from the radio for a minute or two (nothing too long) and write down the gist of what you hear in as much detail as you can. Listen to your recording again and see how accurately you have listened.

Problem 2

You may be distracted by a neighbour coughing or someone knocking a pencil on the floor or some loud noise outside the classroom. Your concentration may simply drift and you will end up in a day-dream.

Solution

Make sure you have enough practice of actual listening exams for a length of time which will give you an idea of what the real exam will be like.

Problem 3

Although there are not many regional variations in vocabulary to trouble you at GCSE, German spoken with an Austrian, Bavarian, Berlin or Swiss accent will sound different and may take a little getting used to. You may also not be used to listening to both male and female voices speaking German.

Solution

Your teacher can help by pointing out such regional differences when they occur in your lessons. Of greatest assistance, however, is satellite television to which many people have access nowadays. Turning on a German TV channel and immersing yourself in a game show or listening to the weather forecast is a very valuable aid to understanding. If you are able to watch like this, it is even better if you can do so at a regular time each week, so that you have the best chance of seeing the same programme.

Problem 4

Understanding a speaker you can't see is a skill you need to practise. You have none of the clues of gesture or facial expression which aid normal understanding.

Solution

You can try it in class by closing your eyes when the teacher is talking to the whole class - but you might warn the teacher first about what you are doing!

Problem 5

The interference between you and the message you are trying to hear may be a deliberately recorded sound effect such a train, or a bell.

Solution

Don't be alarmed. These sound effects are supposed to help you, to put what you hear in some sort of context, so think about them as well.

☀ General strategies

Using the question to help you

■ In multiple-choice questions about simple facts, you know that one answer is correct, so you can go through the answers in your mind before you hear the recording. For example, if the question is:

Eine Fahrkarte kostet: € 4,50 € 5,40 € 15,40 € 15,45?

you can focus on these numbers and disregard everything else.

■ Even if the factual information is slightly more complex, the same still applies, for example:

Eine einfache Fahrkarte nach Bonn-Bad Godesberg kostet:
€ 4,50 € 5,40 € 15,40 € 15,45?

Now you are listening for a particular type of ticket to a specified destination.

■ If the question wants you to focus on an emotion or attitude, think about the words and expressions associated with those emotions, for example:

Maria treibt gern Sport.   RICHTIG   FALSCH?

You should listen out for phrases like *mag gern, interessiert sich für, hat Spaß, findet … gut/schön*. You are unlikely to hear the exact words of the question in the recording.

Using the context to help you

■ *Am Rande des Waldes war ein Teich, in dem Georg immer gern angelte.*

Even without knowing that *ein Teich* means 'a pond', you should be able to work out that it is a stretch of water, because the *angelte* makes it so obvious.

Using your common sense

■ If you are at a petrol station, you are more likely to hear someone say:
Fünfzig Liter Bleifrei, bitte.
than:
Fünfzig Kilo Kartoffeln, bitte.

■ Similarly you should have some idea from your knowledge of German food that a *Bratwurst mit Pommes Frites* is more likely to cost € 4,50 than € 45,00.

▨ Points to practise ▨

☀ Numbers

- You will already be aware of the importance of numbers at Foundation Level - in times, prices and so on - but even at Higher Level there are questions in which an understanding of numbers is crucial.

- Practise counting numbers in English from twenty upwards with the units before the tens, in order to 'tune in' to the German way of counting.

- This becomes increasingly important when listening to telephone numbers, which are usually said as pairs of numbers:
  > 285893: *achtundzwanzig, achtundfünfzig, dreiundneunzig*

  If there is an odd number it is usually left until last:
  > 3572590: *fünfunddreißig, zweiundsiebzig, neunundfünfzig, null*

- Remind yourself of the ordinal numbers by reciting them aloud, especially the first few: *erste, zweite, dritte, vierte*.

- Watch out for the halves: *eineinhalb, zweieinhalb*, etc! *Anderthalb* can also be used for one and a half.

- Be careful with the colloquial expressions of time around the half hour:
  > 2.30 *halb drei*
  > 2.20 *zehn vor halb drei*
  > 2.25 *fünf vor halb drei*
  > 2.35 *fünf nach halb drei*
  > 2.40 *zehn nach halb drei*

☀ Vowels and consonants

- German speakers avoid confusion between similar sounds by making them clearly different from one another. For example, if someone wants to make it clear over the phone that they are talking about June and not July, they will say *Juno*. Or they might say *Julei* instead of *Juli*. Similarly, *zwei* and *drei* are differentiated by using *zwo* instead of *zwei* as necessary.

- Most of us tend to visualise the words we hear in our 'mind's eye', rather like the autocue that a newsreader uses. German is largely written as you would expect. There are no hidden sounds and everything is pronounced. Just one or two sounds might confuse this pattern, such as the 'b' at the end of words like *halb*, or the 'd' which sounds like a 't' at the end of *Hund*. Similarly, the 's' of *See* might make you think the word you hear is *Zeh*, or that *so* is in fact *Zoo*.

- Other vowels to listen for are:

  ä – which can sound like an 'e'. Can you differentiate between *Rädern* and *reden*?

  ü – in *Tür*. Can you hear the difference between *Tour, Tür* and *Tier*? Or between *für* und *vier*? The context in which the words are heard will definitely help you.

☀ Negatives

- *Nicht* is an obvious sound to listen out for, but you can be caught out by *nicht wahr*, when the sentence is, in fact, positive:

  Das Wetter ist schön, nicht wahr?

  The intonation of the question ending should help you to understand this sentence.

- Far more prevalent, and a constant cause of problems, is the *kein/klein* trap:

  Ich habe einen kleinen Garten./Ich habe keinen Garten.

  Even if you miss the sound of the 'l' in *kleinen*, you should still hear the article before *klein*, which you will not hear in front of *kein*, because it already means 'not a' or 'no'.

☀ Word separation

- Without seeing the gaps between words, as you can when you read, it can be difficult to distinguish the beginnings and ends of words.

- Practise listening to a relatively easy piece of German from early in your course book and try to write down what you hear from the recording. You should be able to pick out plenty of shorter words and probably fill in some of the longer ones. If you can borrow the cassette with a transcript of the recording, you will be able to check your spelling as well. Even without this, it is still good practice.

Higher Level performance

At Higher Level, you will be expected to be able to do a number of things which are not expected at Foundation Level.

Understanding German spoken at normal speed

At Foundation Level, the German you are likely to hear will be spoken more slowly and deliberately. At Higher Level, you should expect to hear German spoken at near normal speed, appropriate to the situation, and in some cases containing colloquial language or slang.

Extracting information from longer utterances

At Foundation Level, there is little extra language included beyond what you need for the answer. For example, you might be asked about the weather tomorrow from the extract:
> *Morgen wird das Wetter wieder schön.*

At Higher Level, you are likely to hear a relatively large amount of language from which you have to extract the answer. For example, you might hear:
> *Morgen im Süden meist wolkig. Tageshöchsttemperaturen liegen bei 15 Grad. Im Norden wird es wieder schön. Tageshöchsttemperaturen liegen bei 22 Grad.*

and be asked about the weather in the north. In both cases the German you need to understand is the same (*es wird schön*), but at Higher Level you have to sift through more language to get there.

Picking out the main points from what you hear

For example, you might listen to a discussion on what young people want to do in their free time. One might say:
> *Am liebsten möchte ich im See schwimmen gehen.*

Another might say:
> *Man könnte dort auch segeln oder ein Ruderboot mieten.*

While the last might say:
> *Unten am Wasser gefällt's mir am besten.*

You need to understand that all of them are keen on water sports.

Identifying attitudes and opinions

You will not necessarily always hear key words like *langweilig* or *toll* to tell you how people feel. For example:
> *Ich gehe nur ins Theater, wenn meine Eltern bezahlen.*

might show a reluctance to go to the theatre, whereas:
> *Ich habe für die Theaterkarten schon sehr lange Geld gespart.*

would show a strong desire to see the performance.

Making deductions from what you have heard

As an example, if you hear:

> *Unterwegs hatte ich eine Reifenpanne und ich musste eine halbe Stunde*
> *am Straßenrand sitzen, bis ich das Rad repariert hatte.*

you should be able to deduce that the speaker has been out for a cycle ride.

Understanding the gist of what you hear

If you hear someone say:

> *Kein Jugendzentrum, nicht 'mal eine Disco. Ganz wenige*
> *Sportmöglichkeiten. In dieser Stadt gibt es zu wenig für unsere Jugend.*
> *Kein Wunder, dass sie ab und zu dumme Sachen mit Alkohol machen.*

you can deduce that they are talking about problems facing young
people today.

Answering questions using German which you have not heard on the recording

If you had to answer this question about the above utterance:

> *Was hält er von den Freizeitmöglichkeiten in der Stadt?*

you would have to answer:

> *Er findet die Situation schlecht für junge Leute.*

If you simply said what was lacking (no disco, no youth club, etc.) you
would not score the mark. It is the attitude which is being targeted.

Understanding vocabulary outside the minimum core vocabulary

All the exam boards specify a minimum core vocabulary for Foundation
Level, but there will always be words outside the range of the core which
you have not met. You will therefore need to listen beyond the odd words
that you don't recognise for the gist of the whole passage. Needless to say,
the more vocabulary you **do** know the better, so you need to make a long-
term commitment to the regular learning and using of new words. The
Higher Level vocabulary in Revision Session 2, Units 1–13, will help you.

Different kinds of listening

☼ Dialogues

If there is more than one speaker, you need to be clear who is talking. The names are always recorded and may be used by one speaker to another:

- *Wir gehen heute schwimmen. Kommst du mit, Bettina?*
- *Nein, ich habe keine Lust.*

This should make it clear enough that the second speaker is Bettina.

You may be asked to fill information alongside names in a grid, or to tick correct statements about each named speaker.

☼ Monologues

Examples include news items, weather forecasts, advertisements, etc. The question will make it clear who is speaking.

☼ Announcements

These are usually included at Foundation Level only and include the sort of things you hear over a loudspeaker in a shop, railway station, airport, etc. You often need to listen for specific facts like times, prices, platforms, etc.

☼ Telephone calls and recorded messages

Again, the question will often target points like times and dates, but you may need to listen out for a change in arrangements.

☼ Multiple-choice (non-verbal)

This sort of exercise is often called picture-matching. There are three main types:

1   In the simplest sort, you may have to pick out a time or a price from the recording and match it to one of those on the question paper.

2   You may have to match statements to numbered pictures or symbols, for example, those representing people's jobs or interests.

3   You may have to decide upon the most appropriate scene from a longer recording. For example, is the family at the beach, at the theatre or walking in the woods, etc?

In 1 you are listening for a specific detail, whereas in 2 and 3 you need to pick up the gist of an utterance, probably a longer one. In the case of similar pictures to choose from, you will need to focus on the detail of the pictures and decide what differences there are, before you can listen out for them. It might be a different number of people involved, or different weather, for example.

☼ Multiple-choice (verbal)

Again, there are a number of types:

1   One-word answers are fairly straightforward:
       Georg ist _____. (glücklich/traurig/böse/müde)

At Foundation Level you might even hear the missing word required. The more difficult questions often require more deduction.

2   A phrase may be required instead of a single word. These are less likely to be heard exactly as written down:
       Sie treffen sich _____. (am Bahnhof/im Café/in der Schule/vor der Schule)

In this example, the last two choices are very close and you would have to listen closely to differentiate between 'in' and 'in front of the school'.

3   Sentence answers can take two forms. They might ask you to relate one of the choices to a specific person:
       Was machte Ingrid abends?
       A   Sie ging einkaufen.   *C   Sie hörte Musik.*
       B   Sie machte Hausaufgaben.   *D   Sie besuchte Freundinnen.*

Or they might ask you to choose a person for each statement, in which case you will certainly have more people to choose from than there are statements:
       Schreiben Sie den richtigen Namen.
       ... ist ein fleißiger Schüler.   *... fährt gern Rad.*
       ... kann sehr gut Volleyball spielen.   *... sammelt gern Münzen.*

☀ Answers in German

Again, these may ask for one word, a phrase or a whole sentence:

1   If you are writing one-word answers in a grid-filling exercise, the spelling is not usually a problem - unless your mis-spelling happens to create another German word. For example, if the correct answer is *eine Tür*, the examiner would not be able to accept *eine Tour* or *ein Tier* because the answer would mean something different.

2   If you are asked to write a phrase, then a one-word answer is unlikely to score the mark. For example, if the question is: *Wo treffen sich die Freunde?*, the answer *Bahnhof* would not be clear enough to score the mark. You would need to say *am Bahnhof* or *vor dem Bahnhof*, as appropriate.

3   For the highest grades you may be required to write full sentence answers. At the simplest, these are likely to be manipulations of the recording. For example, you might hear someone say *Ich möchte schwimmen gehen*, and for your answer write *Er möchte schwimmen gehen*. However, you might have to create your own sentence in answer to a question like *Was hält Bernd von dem Film?* Here, your answer might be *Er findet den Film/ihn ziemlich spannend* or *Bernd mochte den Film gar nicht*.

☀ Answers in English

It is tempting to think that these are going to be easier than anything involving German, but in fact candidates often prove less reliable or less precise when using their own language. These questions are usually reserved for the most difficult passages and test the greatest understanding, particularly in respect of attitudes and emotions. These questions more frequently ask **how?** and **why?** than **what?** or **where?**

Questions to try

Find Unit 14: Questions to try on the CD (Tracks 1–7). Listen to each item twice, then answer the questions.

SECTION 1   FOUNDATION   25 marks

FOUNDATION

Kreuzen Sie das richtige Kästchen an!

1 In der Jugendherberge fragen Sie nach den Esszeiten. Wann isst man zu Abend?

    A 18.00–20.00 Uhr ☐   **C** 18.30–19.30 Uhr ☐

    B 18.30–20.30 Uhr ☐   **D** 19.00–20.00 Uhr ☐   [1]

2 Was müssen Sie machen, wenn Sie abends später ausbleiben wollen?

    A Einen Schlüssel dalassen. ☐

    B Ihre Eltern anrufen. ☐

    C Den Herbergseltern einen Schlüssel geben. ☐

    D Den Herbergseltern Bescheid sagen. ☐   [1]

3 Wie ist das Wetter im Süden?

    A ☐   **C** ☐

    B ☐   **D** ☐   [1]

4 Wie ist das Wetter im Westen?

    A ☐   **C** ☐

    B ☐   **D** ☐   [1]

5 Wie ist das Wetter im Norden?

    A ☐   **C** ☐

    B ☐   **D** ☐   [1]

6 Temperaturen im Osten?

    A 13–15 Grad ☐   **C** 14–16 Grad ☐

    B 13–16 Grad ☐   **D** 14–17 Grad ☐   [1]

7 Was mag er am liebsten machen?

    A ☐   **C** ☐

    B ☐   **D** ☐   [1]

8 Hören Sie die Anzeige an. Welche Aussagen sind richtig? Kreuzen **zwei** Kästchen an.

    A Die Museen sind heute zu. ☐

    B Alle drei Gruppen besuchen ein Museum oder eine Galerie. ☐

    C Jeder Besucher kann seine Gruppe wählen. ☐

    D Einige Leute besuchen einen Vergnügungspark. ☐

    E Alle Leute essen zusammen zu Mittag. ☐   [2]

9 Hören Sie das Telefongespräch an und korrigieren Sie den folgenden Zettel.

> Lieber Herr Blume,
>
> Frau Teichmann hat für Sie angerufen.
>
> Sie kommt erst um 16.00 Uhr.
>
> Treffpunkt: Vor dem Rathaus

    [4]

Hören Sie die Gespräche an. Wählen Sie für Frank und für Birgit ein passendes Adjektiv.

10 Frank ist…

    A egoistisch ☐   **C** traurig ☐

    B ängstlich ☐   **D** großzügig ☐   [1]

11 Birgit ist…

    A gut gelaunt ☐   **C** böse ☐

    B deprimiert ☐   **D** glücklich ☐   [1]

12 Wo war der Campingplatz?

    A am Strand ☐   **C** nicht weit vom See ☐

    B nicht weit vom Wasser ☐   **D** direkt am See ☐   [1]

13 Wo waren die Eltern? Schreiben Sie den Satz zu Ende.

Die Eltern waren _____   [1]

14 Warum möchte sie auf die Universität gehen?   [1]

15 Warum möchte sie Fremdsprachen studieren?   [1]

Answer the following questions in ENGLISH.

16 Herr Schwarz is talking about his recent holiday.

    a Name two of the problems at the campsite.   [2]

    b What did he decide to do?   [1]

    c Why did his decision not work out at first?   [1]

    d Why might he have felt pleased in the end? Give **two** details.   [2]

[Total for Section 1: 25 marks]

SECTION 2   FOUNDATION AND HIGHER   19 marks

1 **Annas Stundenplan**

Hören Sie das Stück zweimal an!
Listen to the piece twice.

Anna beschreibt ihren Stundenplan.
Anna is describing her timetable.

Füllen Sie den folgenden Stundenplan aus.
Complete the timetable below. You may make notes or write your
answers at any time.   [10]

Stunde	Montag	Dienstag	Mittwoch	Donnerstag	Freitag	Samstag
1	Englisch	Deutsch	Mathe		Biologie	
2	Geschichte		Deutsch	Englisch	Deutsch	Englisch
	P	A	U	S	E	
3		Kunst		Informatik		
4	Musik	Physik				
	P	A	U	S	E	
5	Deutsch		Chemie	Sozialkunde	Englisch	
6		Mathe	Latein	Mathe	Latein	
7		Turnen				
8		Turnen				

---

2 Wie kommt man dahin?

Hören Sie das Stück zweimal an!
Listen to the piece twice.

You may make notes or write your answers at any time.

Sie sind im Verkehrsamt. Sie haben einen Stadtplan und wollen herausfinden, wie man sich in der Stadt zurechtfindet. Von einem Wegweiserautomaten hören Sie die folgenden Hinweise.

Schreiben Sie den passenden Buchstaben in die richtigen Kästchen. Sie brauchen nicht alle Kästchen.

You are in the tourist office. You have a town plan and want to find out how to get to certain important places. From a machine you hear the directions to nine places twice each with a pause between each playing.

Write the correct letter in the appropriate box on the map. You do not need all the boxes.   [9]

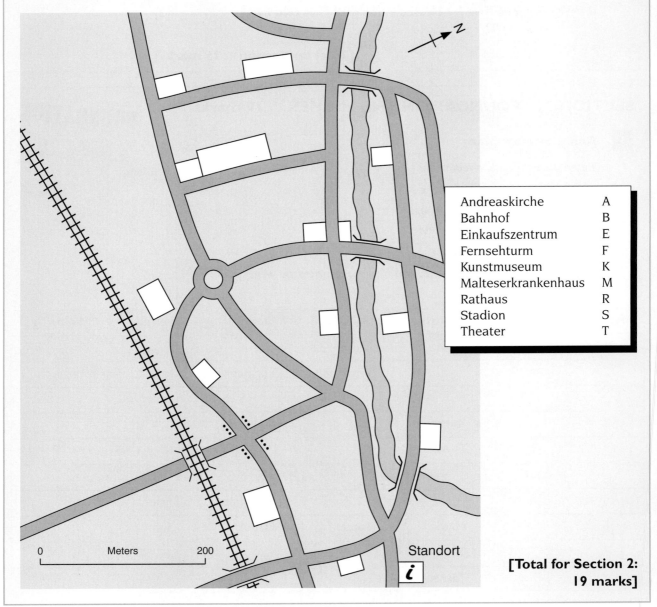

Andreaskirche	A
Bahnhof	B
Einkaufszentrum	E
Fernsehturm	F
Kunstmuseum	K
Malteserkrankenhaus	M
Rathaus	R
Stadion	S
Theater	T

0   Meters   200

Standort

[Total for Section 2: 19 marks]

SECTION 3   HIGHER   19 marks

1   **Im Fundbüro**

Hören Sie das Stück zweimal an!
Listen to the piece twice.

Ergänzen Sie die Sätze mit den passenden Wörtern!
Complete the sentences with the appropriate words or phrases.

1   Das Mädchen ging ins Fundbüro, _____.

    um Geld zu holen
    um Informationen zu bekommen
    um etwas zu finden

2   Sie hatte die Jacke **a** _____

    b _____ verloren.

    a am Tag davor   **b** auf der Straße
       letzte Woche   im Kino
       morgen   im Park

3   Die Jacke war _____ und

    _____.

    dreckig   teuer
    neu   nicht mehr neu
    groß   hellblau

4   In der Tasche der Jacke hatte das Mädchen _____

    und _____.

    eine Fahrkarte   ihre Schlüssel
    etwas Geld   Bonbons
    ein Foto

5   Das Mädchen hat _____ zurückgekriegt.

    alles
    nichts
    nur eine Sache   [8]

2 *Hören Sie das Stück zweimal an!*
Listen to the piece twice.

Wer ist das? Schreiben Sie die folgenden Namen in die fünf richtigen Kästchen.
Drei Kästchen werden leer bleiben. [5]

Peter	Gerd	Martin	Norbert	Jürgen

Schreiben Sie die Namen							
		✓	✓				✓
	✓	✓				✓	
	✓		✓			✓	
			✓		✓	✓	
	✓	✓			✓		
			✓	✓			✓
	✓				✓	✓	
			✓	✓			✓

3 *Hören Sie das Stück zweimal an!*
Listen to the piece twice.

Kreuzen Sie die vier richtigen Sätze an!

1 Die Wettervorhersage kommt am Freitag im Radio. ☐
2 In den letzten Tagen war es etwas kälter als jetzt. ☐
3 Die erste Nacht bleibt trocken. ☐
4 Es wird am Samstag Eis auf den Straßen geben. ☐
5 Das Tiefdruckgebiet kommt vom Süden. ☐
6 Am Samstag sieht man im Süden keine Sonne. ☐
7 Am Samstagabend könnte es im Norden stürmisch werden. ☐
8 Es gibt fast keinen Wind. ☐ [4]

4 *Hören Sie das Stück zweimal an!*
Listen to the piece twice.

Ergänzen Sie die folgenden Sätze!
Complete the following sentences.

1 Bernd will nicht gleich Fußball spielen, weil …
2 Er will mitgehen, wenn …
3 Bernd geht ins Kino, nachdem …
4 Ralf bekommt den 'Gameboy', bevor …
5 Bernds Familie macht jetzt Urlaub, damit … [5]

[Total for Section 3: 22 marks]

You will find the transcripts and answers, with examiner's comments, on pages 156–66.

REVISION SESSION 1

How to overcome problems

Unlike in the Listening Test, you have a large degree of control over what you say or choose not to say during the Speaking Test. You have probably been taught to recognise different ways of expressing the same thing in German, but for the purposes of the Speaking Test, it is important that you routinely use the same way of saying, for example, 'Thank you' or 'Excuse me'. It simply makes good sense to reduce the number of things that you need to think about.

In the General Conversation you have a great opportunity to steer the course of the exam and to tell the examiner, your teacher, all the things you have prepared. Of course the examiner needs to probe the depth of your ability, and to find out how you can respond to material which you have not prepared.

If your Speaking Test includes a presentation, the choice of topic is yours, and it presents you with a good chance to show your preparation.

☀ Problems and solutions

Problem 1

Most candidates experience a degree of nervousness before the exam. You will probably worry about making a fool of yourself by mispronouncing a word, or by forgetting a simple word or phrase just when you need it. However, it is a real bonus to have a familiar face as the examiner, so make the most of your teacher's experience!

Solution

Your teacher will have talked you through the stages of the exam in the months and weeks preceding the test, and you should have had some practice with exam materials. Always use a tape recorder when practising. Don't just look through a role-play in your bedroom and imagine how you will do it. Turn off the music, press the 'RECORD' button and speak up. Of course it sounds funny at first, but you will soon get used to the sound of your own voice. Try reading a paragraph of a simple text out loud, and get used to the pitch and volume which makes the best recording.

Problem 2

You are so well-prepared that you want to rush through a lot in a short time. Your level of concentration is such that you stare straight past the examiner at the wall behind, creating the impression that you are reading from an invisible auto-cue like a newsreader. It can also lead to a problem if the examiner wants to ask a question out of interest, or to check your understanding of the topic.

Solution

When you make your recordings, speak slowly and clearly, leaving an occasional pause of two or three seconds. These are the pauses which allow the examiner to take in what you are saying and to give you credit for it. Make eye contact with the examiner, so that your facial expression helps with the meaning. Your experienced teacher can read your enthusiasm in your face as well as hearing about your hobbies and interests.

Problem 3

Too long a gap in your speaking can become a worry for both you and the examiner. Have you forgotten what to say? Have you understood the examiner's question? It could spoil the fluency which you are trying to achieve.

Solution

If you pause while you think of your favourite food or pastime, this is only natural, but try to have an answer ready for most of the obvious questions such as these. They are almost entirely predictable. You may be forgiven for drawing breath while considering something less predictable in the Higher role-play, but you can use a well-timed *ich weiß nicht* to stall for time; at least the examiner knows you are still working on it!

Problem 4

You finally come up against a difficulty which you can't deal with: either you do not know what the examiner is asking, or you do not know how to answer, perhaps because you are lacking a key word in German.

Solution

In the first case you need to let the examiner know as soon as possible that you are in difficulty. Your eye contact will already have betrayed a lack of comprehension, but for the sake of the person who will later listen to the recording, you need to say what is wrong.

■ If the problem is general, then *Ich verstehe nicht* will move the situation along. This is slightly better than *Können Sie das wiederholen?*, because if the examiner repeats the same words exactly, you may be no further forward. The likelihood is that the examiner will see your predicament and re-phrase the question for you.

■ If there is one German word that you don't recognise you should say *Ich verstehe das Wort (German word) nicht*, or *Was heißt (German word)?* which may also lead to some easier re-phrasing. In either case you will have retrieved the situation, which is to your credit even if you gain no marks for the odd word you don't know.

■ If you've forgotten a key word for an answer, simply say *Ich habe das Wort für (English word) vergessen*. Your teacher can 'feed' you the word and you can continue without drying up. You may get no credit for that particular sentence, but you do gain credit for coping with the difficulty in as natural a way as possible.

Problem 5

You may forget what you have rehearsed or the order in which to make your points, resulting in confusion for you or the examiner.

Solution

You may be allowed to make notes on the role-plays, and you should be allowed to take some cue-cards into the exam room to assist your presentation. For the role-plays a note will help you remember what you want to say, and for the presentation the cards help you to maintain your intended order. As a rule, you should limit yourself to single words or short phrases, and not try to write every word you want to say.

■ Hints on pronunciation ■

☀ The alphabet

You may have to spell out your name or a place in a role-play or general conversation. Find Unit 15: The alphabet on the CD (Track 8) and listen to the German alphabet. Here is a guide to the pronunciation:

A	ah	H	hah	O	oh	U	oo
B	bay	I	ee	P	pay	V	fow
C	say	J	yot	Q	koo	W	vay
D	day	K	kah	R	air	X	icks
E	ay	L	ell	S	ess	Y	ipsilon
F	eff	M	emm	T	tay	Z	tsed
G	gay	N	enn				

Notice also the following:

ß – sounds like 'ss'.

s – sounds like an English 'z'.

z – is unknown in English, but sounds as if you are saying a 't' before an 's': *Tsimmer*.

If you have to say two of the same letter, simply say *Doppel-ess* for 'ss', etc.

☀ Vowel sounds

■ **au** – sounds like 'ow' in cow, or like 'ou' in loud.

■ The following two sounds are very common but are frequently mixed up:

    ie – sounds like 'ee' as in reed.

    ei – sounds like 'i' as in ride.

If in doubt, simply say the second of the two letters in English to remind you which is which.

■ The following vowels occur with the umlaut or 'sound shift' to modify their sound. The English sound is only very approximate so you may need to ask for further guidance from your teacher, or practise them with your language assistant.

    ä – is more like the English 'a' as in gate.

    ö – is like the sound of disgust you might make when you spot something you don't like the look of!

    ü – is more like the English 'ea' or 'ee' than 'oo', so try saying *Brüder* like 'breeder'.

REVISION SESSION 3 — How to tackle role-plays

These test your ability to negotiate a transaction. In simple terms, this means you have to:

- buy something
- ask directions
- make an arrangement
- use a public service such as a bank, or post office or a combination of these.

The Higher Level role-plays are slightly more complex and often put you in situations where you need to respond to the unexpected, but even this can be prepared. The OCR Higher role-play is a little different, in that it asks you to describe a series of events, such as a day trip, and the situations are often very similar to those in the Higher Level writing.

The boards will often use symbols, plus a **?** to show that **you** have to ask a question. You might also meet the following phrases:

Sie beginnen	
Wählen Sie	*Buchstabieren Sie*
Bestellen Sie	*Erklären Sie*
Beschreiben Sie	*Bezahlen Sie*
Fragen Sie nach…	*Machen Sie einen Vorschlag*
Sagen Sie	*Beantworten Sie*
Geben Sie	*Grüßen Sie*

Ask your teacher to check all the above details for your board.

Foundation

The tasks will be presented in English, usually with some visuals.

Preparation
- Remember: the instructions tell you what the task is. You must **not** translate the instructions into German. For example, if the instruction tells you to ask your friend what he wants to drink, you don't need the German for 'ask' or 'friend'. Simply say *Was möchtest du trinken?*

- Think through what you will say for each task. You might even be able to say it quietly to yourself as you sit in the preparation area.

- The teacher will start the role-play unless you are told otherwise.

- You should not need to understand what the teacher says in order to fulfil your tasks.

- Make notes if you are allowed to, but don't then read them like a script.

- Don't spend too long on the first Foundation task; you will need to save your preparation time for the harder tasks.

In the test
- Be calm – you have done your preparation and you still have the instructions in front of you.

Foundation/Higher

At this level, there will always be something unpredictable to deal with, so read the instructions through carefully. Again, the scene is set in English, but the tasks are in German.

Preparation
- Try to guess what the unpredictable element might be. It can often be something as simple as a time, or a spelling, which is required.

In the test
- Remember your eye contact. Look at the examiner when the unpredictable element is due, and you should understand more easily what is required.

Higher

Most of these role-plays will contain a problem for you to solve, or something for you to negotiate – they will not be straightforward. The OCR Higher role-play will ask you to describe a series of events in the past tense.

Preparation
- You need to think through the situation as set out on the card, and explore some of the avenues which might open up as the conversation develops. Remember, you can't prepare a script in advance. This role-play is really a series of unpredictable questions and ad lib responses on your part.

- For example, if you are returning goods to a shop you will need to think of the reasons why you might do so. Are the goods broken or damaged? Do you want to change the colour/size of clothes? Are you asking politely or complaining bitterly? What tone will you adopt?

In the test
- Maintain eye contact and respond appropriately to the examiner.

- Make sure that you are true to the situation on the card and give any information accurately as set down.

Higher (OCR)

Remember to use the past tense – perfect for the actions and imperfect (simple past) for the weather and moods.

Preparation
- The most important thing is to work out the sequence of pictures and look at the time-scale. It will usually be a day's events, so you can almost certainly use easy vocabulary to describe daily routine like getting up, having breakfast, leaving the house, travelling to school/town, lunch, evening meal, time for bed, etc.

- Try to think of something to say about each picture, remembering to mention how the characters might feel. You are usually offered the choice of telling the story in the 1st person (i.e. you or you and your friend are the main characters), or you can tell it in the 3rd person (saying 'he did this' and 'they did that'). You should feel much more secure in the 1st person.

- The OCR cards always contain helpful vocabulary, individual words and sometimes phrases under each picture. Use these with care. Don't simply read them out. They may be questions which are intended to prompt you. For example:

    Wohin gefahren?

Make sure you handle the verb correctly and say:

    Ich bin/Wir sind in die Stadt gefahren.

    Was gemacht?
    Wir haben Volleyball gespielt.

Say whether you enjoyed it or not, or how you felt.

    Wir haben viel Spaß gehabt. Es hat mir gut gefallen.

In the test

- Keep one eye on the card so that you don't lose the sequence, but make sure you try to interest the examiner in what you are saying. You might even try something humorous, if you feel confident enough. After all, some of the pictures may well lead you to the conclusion that something funny has happened. For example:
  – Georg has put on Udo's trousers after swimming and looks very silly because they don't fit.
  – Margret has found a great skirt to buy but gets to the counter and finds that she has no money.
  A laugh during the test will do you good!

How to tackle Presentation and Discussion

Presentation and Discussion forms part of the Speaking Test for both OCR and AQA and may be used as coursework for Edexcel (London). Go on to the next section if you use a different exam board.

You need to speak for 1 minute (OCR) or 1¹/₂ minutes (AQA) on a topic you choose from one of the areas of experience. Then your teacher will ask you some questions about your Presentation.

Choosing your topic

You may choose something you know very well, such as *Meine Schule* or *Meine Familie*, or talk about *Mein Hobby*, *Mein Urlaub* or *Mein Schulaustausch*. Make sure you check the choice of topic with your teacher first and listen to his/her advice, as the choice might restrict the mark you get in the test.

■ If you choose a basic topic and talk in simple sentences, you may simply not cover enough ground to raise your mark into the Higher Level range. Simple sentences, simple opinions and present tense will not add up to a good mark. Conversely, if you choose a difficult or obscure topic, you may grind to a halt for lack of vocabulary in German.

■ Discuss your Presentation with your teacher so that he/she can prepare sensible questions to ask you.

■ Introduce the topic in the first sentence for the benefit of the examiner who will listen to the cassette later and who has no prior knowledge of the topic.

How much detail

Say enough to make the topic interesting, but don't try to impress the examiner with everything you know about the subject in detail. This is not the purpose of the test.

■ Avoid lists of more than a few words. On no account should you, for example, try to list all your teachers in school, or all the teams you've played against!

■ Try to avoid English words and expressions. It is better to say *Ich höre gern englische Popmusik* than to say *Ich höre gern Oasis*. If you are describing your favourite TV viewing, then stick to a general term like *Sportsendungen*, rather than saying *Match of the Day* or *Grandstand*.

■ Make sure you have planned a few sentences in the past and future. This is essential to your scoring well, and even the simplest sentences can do the trick: *Letztes Jahr hat unsere Mannschaft einen Pokal gewonnen* or *Wir werden nächstes Jahr sicherlich besser spielen*.

■ Time what you are preparing so that you don't run too far over time or, worse still, don't fill up the allotted time.

Cue cards

These are vital to stop you forgetting what you want to say and to maintain the order.

- Key words or short phrases are all you need. You are not allowed to bring in a script to read from.

- Don't have too many.

- Number them.

- Don't read from them.

Delivery

Practise regularly beforehand what you are going to say and make a recording of it so you get used to the sound of your voice.

- You don't need to be word perfect. It usually doesn't sound as good, your voice becomes monotonous, and you lose the real communication with the person you should be talking to.

- Don't try to rush. You may trip yourself up or miss vital points. Remember how long you have spent preparing for this one minute.

- If you are allowed to bring in visual aids such as a photograph or an object (no pet reptiles!), this can be a help to you and the examiner, but choose these carefully, and don't simply pick a photo of a lot of people and then list who they all are. Try to pick something which can lead to a bit more discussion after you have done your Presentation.

Predicting the questions

- Leave something for the teacher to ask you. You can deliberately leave out saying something obvious like where you stayed on holiday, so that the teacher can make a note of it and come back to the question in the discussion which follows.

- Remind yourself of the German question words *Was? Wann? Was für?*, etc. (see Unit 10). Go through your Presentation and stop frequently and think which question word would be sensible at any point. This is probably what is going through the examiner's mind when you give your Presentation.

■ How to tackle General ■ Conversation

This is the common test of all boards, although there are minor variations in what each one requires. Make sure you understand clearly from your teacher what to do. This is your big chance to show what you can do, and the topics are all familiar to you.

Tenses

You will not achieve a Grade C unless you can show knowledge of the past, present and future tenses. Your teacher is obliged to make the opportunities available to you and you need to listen out for your 'prompts':

Was hast du letztes Wochenende gemacht?
Wo warst du letzten Sommer in den Ferien? (for the past tenses)
Was wirst du im September machen?
Was hast du nächstes Jahr vor? (for the future)

These are obvious introductions which you will probably practise with your teacher beforehand.

Opinions

Apart from the use of *gern* with simple verb phrases, how will you express what you feel about things? Try some of the following if you want to make an impression:

Ich glaube, dass…	I think that…
Ich meine, dass es besser sein könnte.	I think it could be better.
Meiner Meinung nach ist das die beste Mannschaft.	In my opinion they're the best team.
Ich halte das für dumm.	I think it's stupid.
Ich habe es satt.	I'm fed up with it.

Remember, you need to express opinions for your Grade C.

Full accounts and descriptions

■ Try to link ideas and sentences using conjunctions such as *denn, aber, dann.*

■ Impress the examiner with a relative clause or two, using the relative pronouns *der, die, das* (see Unit 9).

■ Think about some more adventurous adjectives and adverbs to add interest to your comments.

■ Take every opportunity to expand on a question. Don't 'close down' the possibilities by a *ja/nein* or other brief answer. So, for example, when asked, *Hast du Geschwister?*, instead of just *Ja* or *Ja, zwei Schwestern*, you should continue with some further details: *Die eine heißt Susie und die andere Margaret. Sie sind beide älter als ich und studieren schon auf der Uni.*

What not to do

■ Don't allow pauses to go on too long, or hesitate before every answer.

■ Don't make the teacher work hard to get you to talk.

■ Don't clam up for fear of making a mistake. You don't have to be word perfect to get the message across.

Questions to try

Aim to spend no more than 2–3 minutes preparing a Foundation or Foundation/Higher role-play, and 5–6 minutes preparing a Higher role-play. In the case of the Higher, your preparation must include trying to predict what the examiner might ask you.

SECTION 1   FOUNDATION

 Then find Unit 15: Questions to try on the CD (Tracks 9–11) and compare the recorded answers with what you have prepared.

1   **Im Hotel**   Sie wollen mit Ihrer Familie im Hotel übernachten.

Situation   You and your family want to stay overnight in a German hotel.

Your teacher will play the part of the hotel receptionist and will begin the conversation.

1

2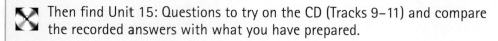

3

4   × 5

5

2   You and your friend are at a café and want to order. Choose two items for each of you from those in the box below. Don't forget to find out where the toilets are, and to start and finish the conversation politely.

1

2   1.....
     2.....

3   3.....
     4.....

4   ?

5

SECTION 2   FOUNDATION AND HIGHER

1   In der Bank

Situation   You have run out of money while in Germany and go into a bank to change some of your travellers' cheques. Your teacher will play the part of the bank clerk and will start the conversation.

1   You have travellers' cheques. What do you say?
2   Say what sort of travellers' cheques you have.
3   Answer the question.
4   You have forgotten your passport. What do you say?
5   Ask about the opening times of the bank.

2   Am Bahnhof

Situation   You are on holiday in Germany and want to visit your friend in Bonn. You go to the railway station to find out about train times and buy a ticket. Your teacher will play the part of the ticket office clerk and start the conversation.

1 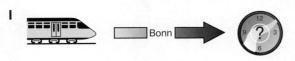 Bonn

2 ← → 3 ! 4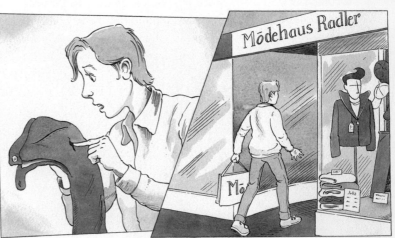

SECTION 3   HIGHER

1   Situation

You have bought some trousers at a clothes shop in town, but when you get back to your youth hostel you realise they have a small tear in them. You take them back the following day. The examiner will start the conversation.

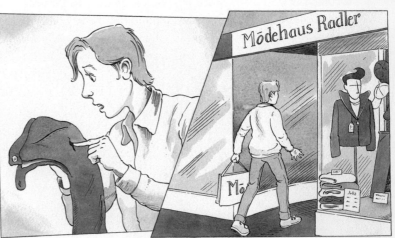

Modehaus Radler

2 **Situation** The notes below give an outline of an exchange visit to Germany you made with your school. Tell the examiner about the journey from your town to Düsseldorf. Be prepared to respond to any questions or comments from the examiner.

Wann abgefahren?	Wie gefahren?		Durchfahrt interessant?

Was gemacht?	Wann angekommen?	Gastfamilie getroffen	Was gegessen?	Müde?

☼ Presentation and Discussion

Prepare a presentation of about 1½ minutes about your family. Begin your presentation with *Ich werde meine Familie beschreiben*.

Then find the appropriate point on the CD (Track 12) and listen to the sample presentation. Did you find similar things to say? Did you include a range of tenses and structures? Did you anticipate the questions the teacher was likely to ask?

☼ General Conversation

Find Track 13 on the CD. Listen to the questions which begin this section and answer as fully as you can. The topics covered are School, Home Town, and Free Time and Leisure. Remember to listen carefully to the tense and respond accordingly. Then listen to the sample student's answer and compare it with what you have said.

You will find transcripts of the sample answers, with examiner's comments, on pages 167–72.

■ How to overcome problems ■

☼ Problems and solutions

It is difficult to separate the four skills. Your grasp of vocabulary and basic language structures play a vital role in helping you to understand written German, but there are specific difficulties associated with reading which can be addressed separately. This unit will help you to identify ways in which you can improve your comprehension of written German.

IMPORTANT NOTE
The tests and texts of the Reading exam paper are composed almost entirely of words within a limited, known and published vocabulary. Your teacher will have this in a pamphlet issued by the exam board. You may already have referred to it in class.

Problem 1
You may be distracted by the style of the print, or any handwriting. Perhaps there are different fonts and sizes of print, or the passage is in newspaper columns.

Solution
Make sure you have enough practice of actual test materials in varying styles. Don't be afraid to pick up a German magazine or newspaper and glance at the advertisements, headlines, or lead paragraphs. Every little helps!

Problem 2
Speed-reading or 'skimming' can cause you to miss the meaning of words you should know, or you mistake them for another word which appears similar.

Solution
Take your time to read words carefully enough. Check the meaning of a word, if you think it may be the key word needed for the understanding of a phrase or sentence.

Problem 3
It can be easy to misunderstand the crucial first word of a question.

Solution
Learn these interrogatives NOW!

Wo?	means	'Where?' not 'Who?'
Wer?	means	'Who?' not 'Where?' This is an unforgivable mistake, even when you are under pressure.
Was?		What?
Wann?		When? (general or specific)

Um wie viel Uhr?	At what time? (specific)
Wie lange?	How long (for)?
Was für ...?	What sort of ...?
Wie viel?	How much?/How many?
Warum?	Why?

Problem 4

You have practised lots of tests which require you to tick boxes for *richtig* or *falsch*, but you will not see these any longer in the Reading paper.

Solution

Look out for the exercises which offer three or four answers or sentences and say *Kreuzen Sie die richtige Antwort* or *die richtigen Antworten an!* You are being asked to tick the correct answer or sentence, and therefore not to tick the other options. The essence of this exercise is the same as you have practised, so don't be fooled by the layout.

☀ General strategies

Using the question to help you

- In multiple-choice questions about simple facts, you know that one answer is correct, so you can bear this in mind when reading the passage. For example, if the question is:

    Eine Rückfahrkarte für einen Fünfzehnjährigen kostet:
    € 15,00   € 10,00   € 7,50   € 5,00 ?

    you can focus on these facts and disregard everything else.

    NOTE: Exam boards do not want to test your mathematical ability. If you find yourself adding up or dividing by two, you are on the wrong track.

- Similarly, if the question wants you to focus on an emotion or attitude, you can look for words and expressions associated with it.
    Statement: *Maria treibt gern Sport.*

    Do you think this is correct? You are unlikely to see the exact same words of that statement in the text, so watch for *mag gern, interessiert sich für, hat Spaß, findet... gut/schön*, and so on.

- Very occasionally, however, you may meet a test which uses three columns. The text tells you that Maria enjoys English and Art. Her brother is a sports teacher, but there is no mention of Maria and sport.

    If you really cannot find the evidence to support either *richtig* or *falsch*, then you may need to tick this third box.

	RICHTIG	FALSCH	NICHT IM TEXT
Maria treibt gern Sport.			✓

Using the context to help you

■ *Auf dem Markt wollte Peter ein Kilo Kirschen kaufen.*

Even without knowing that *Kirschen* are cherries, you should be able to work out that it is something which you can buy in kilos at the market because *Markt*, *Kilo* and *kaufen* are so obvious. Surely you couldn't write 'churches' now!

Using your common sense

■ If you are in a supermarket you are more likely to see a sign which says *Frische Brötchen* than *Ausfahrt freilassen*.

■ Similarly, you should have some idea from your knowledge of German food and drink that a *Bratwurst mit Pommes Frites* is something you eat and so could not be the answer to the question *Was hat Georg getrunken?*

☼ Numbers and time

- Watch out for the following expressions:

eineinhalb (OR *anderthalb*)	one and a half
viereinhalb	four and a half
eine Viertelstunde	a quarter of an hour
eine Dreiviertelstunde	three quarters of an hour
halb zehn	half past nine (Remember the trap!)

☼ Some regular problems for unwary candidates

- See

  The word has two genders and two meanings. Because Germany has so little coastline, but the Germans enjoy watersports so much, you can guess it usually means 'lake'. However, there's no substitute for learning it:

  der See   lake   **die** See   sea

  Phrases such as *am See* show that the noun cannot be feminine and therefore must be 'lake'. Also, don't forget that *das Meer* is more common than *die See*.

- *Die Küche/der Kuchen*

  These two words with food connections can catch you out. If you are unsure, look them up now!

- The *kein/klein* trap

  Enough said? Do you remember the examples from Unit 14?

- There are other problems involving words which look similar but mean quite different things. A dictionary can help you in such cases, if you think you know which meaning you are looking for.

☼ Negatives

- The negatives *gar nicht/gar kein* and *überhaupt nicht/überhaupt kein* are obvious enough, but watch out for *fast*, which means 'almost', and can change the whole meaning of the sentence:

  Er hat den Bus fast verpasst.

  Did he catch the bus or not? Yes, he did.

- Similarly, *nur* can change the whole meaning. *Das kostet nur zwanzig Euro* suggests something is cheap, while *Ich habe nur zehn Euro* suggests that 10 euros is not enough for your needs.

☼ Word separation

■ German is well known for its long compound nouns. Have no fear!
Remember the saying: 'Inside every long word there are short words
trying to get out!' Look at the end of a long noun to find out what the
main noun is. It may be something as simple as *Tisch* or *Wagen*. The
words attached to the front of it describe it in some way or other.

☼ Capital letters

■ These help you to identify the nouns, but may also mislead you into thinking
that a common noun is a place or person. For example, if you see the sentence:
   Man rief den Arzt an, weil die Frau Hilfe brauchte.

don't amuse the examiner by talking about *Frau Hilfe*!

At Higher Level, you will be expected to be able to do a number of things which are not expected at Foundation Level.

Picking out the main points from a passage

You have read the rubric. When you read the questions, remember that they follow the passage chronologically. More importantly, there will not be masses of material in the passage which is not tested. The examiners might set one or two questions per paragraph, but it is unusual for there to be a paragraph which has no question set about it.

Use the paragraph structure of longer passages to help you, and look for key words. Make sure you identify the subject and verb of each sentence, and try to decide which might be key words.

Identifying attitudes and opinions

You will not necessarily always see the key words like *glücklich* or *böse* to tell you how people feel. For example, the sentence:
   Ich bin gern ins Theater gegangen.

will tell you that someone enjoyed the experience, whereas:
   Wenn ich mit meinem Bruder Karten spiele, gibt es immer Ärger!

might suggest a less pleasant atmosphere.

Making deductions/inferences from what you read

If you read:
   Wir haben ziemlich lange auf die Post gewartet, was sehr ungewöhnlich war.

you should be able to deduce that the postman is normally punctual.

Understanding the gist of what you read

If you read:
   Ziemlich viele meiner Klassenkameraden fahren weg, oder machen einen Campingurlaub irgendwo in der Nähe. Nur ich muss die drei Wochen zu Hause bleiben. Aber im Winter mache ich einen Skiurlaub.

you should be able to see that the writer is talking about holidays.

Answering questions using German which you have not heard on the recording

If you had to answer this question about the previous example:
   Was hält sie davon, dass sie jetzt nicht in Urlaub fährt?

you would have to answer:
   Sie ist traurig, dass sie nicht wegfährt. Sie freut sich schon auf ihren Winterurlaub.

If you simply said that she is not going on holiday now, or that she is going in winter, you would not score the mark. It is her feeling about the situation which is being targeted.

◼ Different kinds of reading ◼

☀ Newspaper and magazine articles

These are usually factual and invariably in the past, because the events they describe have already happened. These accounts will be written largely in the imperfect tense, so you need to recognise the verbs quickly. Check the common strong and irregular ones in the verb table in Unit 18 (pages 137–9).

☀ Advertisements

Just as in English, there are no rules of grammar for advertisers, so you may find bold imperatives or questions, or simply statements made without a verb:

> *Nie so was gesehen? Greifen Sie zu! Kaufen Sie sofort das Neueste von VW!*

☀ Descriptive passages

These can range from simple accounts about a school trip to tourist brochures which describe the sights of the area you are visiting. Adjectives will play an important part in setting the tone, so think about the mood of the writing as you read. You are unlikely to encounter negative descriptions in a tourist brochure, nor usually in accounts about a holiday, unless things obviously went wrong. If something is good or bad, there is often a clause nearby to tell you why:

> *Der Urlaub war fantastisch – zwei Wochen lang ununterbrochene Sonne!*

You may never have encountered *ununterbrochen* but it should be obvious that the sun shone a lot.

> *Die Rückfahrt war eine Katastrophe – stundenlang im Auto in der heißen Sonne!*

What comment does the writer make about the sun this time? Certainly not as pleased to see it as the first writer.

■ Different kinds of question ■

☼ Multiple choice (non-verbal)

This sort of exercise is often called picture-matching. These are the three forms:

1 In the simplest sort, you may have to pick out a time or a price from the text and match it to one of those on the question paper.

2 You may have to match statements to numbered pictures or symbols, for example, those representing people's jobs or interests.

3 You may have to decide upon the most appropriate scene from a longer passage. For example, is the family at the beach, at the theatre, or walking in the woods?

In 1, you are reading for a specific detail, whereas in 2 and 3 you need to pick up the gist of a longer passage. In the case of similar pictures to choose from, you will need to focus on the detail of the pictures and decide what differences there are, before you can search for them in the text. There might be a different number of people involved, for example, or different weather.

☼ Multiple choice (verbal)

Again, there are different types:

1 At Foundation Level one-word answers are fairly straightforward:
   Georg ist _____ . (glücklich/traurig/böse/müde)

   However, the more difficult questions often require more deduction.

2 A phrase may be required instead of a single word. These are less likely to be taken directly from the passage.
   *Sie treffen sich _____ . (am Bahnhof/im Café/in der Schule/
   vor der Schule)*

   In this example, the last two choices are very close and you would have to look closely to differentiate between 'in' and 'in front of' the school.

3 Sentence answers. These might ask you to relate one of the choices to a specific person:
   Was machte die Mutter am Nachmittag?
   A *Sie ging einkaufen.*
   B *Sie musste arbeiten.*
   C *Sie hörte Musik.*
   D *Sie besuchte ihre Mutter.*

   Or they might ask you to choose a person for each statement, in which case you will certainly have more people to choose from than there are statements:
   Schreiben Sie den richtigen Namen.
   ...faulenzt sehr gern.
   ...kann sehr gut Schach spielen.
   ...schwimmt mehrmals in der Woche.
   ...kauft gern neue Kleidung.

☀ Answers in German

Some of the above examples are simple ways of making you write German answers. Spelling errors should not occur, because you will simply be copying a word or phrase from the question paper. If you have to write some original German to express your answer, make it as simple as possible to get the point across. Communication is everything; your German is unlikely to be penalised unless it is unclear what you mean.

☀ Answers in English

These questions are usually reserved for the most difficult passages, and test the greatest understanding, particularly where they concern attitudes and emotions which you might struggle to describe in German. These questions more frequently ask **how?** and **why?** than **what?** or **where?** Answers in English are inherently more dangerous in the Reading Test, because you have longer to study the passage and may want to keep adding to your first thought. The danger of a longer answer is that you may obscure your correct thought with other material which could lose you the mark. Only write more than the minimum if your answer becomes clearer. **Always check your answer does not contain contradictory statements.**

■ Questions to try ■

Reading (**Foundation**) consists of **Section 1** and **Section 2**. Reading (**Higher**) consists of **Section 2** and **Section 3**. The following questions are typical of what will be set under the new syllabus: Section 1 – Foundation Tier – multiple choice – mostly visual.

SECTION I   FOUNDATION   18 marks

FOUNDATION

Questions 1–6: Answer each question by ticking one box only.

1 You are in Germany. You need petrol for the car and see the following signs. Which one should you follow?

A Supermarkt ☐   C Gymnasium ☐

B Parkplatz ☐   D Tankstelle ☐   [1]

2 You want to find the town centre. Which sign do you follow?

A Rathaus ☐   C Stadtmitte ☐

B Bahnhof ☐   D Kunstmuseum ☐   [1]

3 You want to buy some bread. Which sign do you look for?

A Metzgerei ☐   C Zeitungen ☐

B Schuhgeschäft ☐   D Bäckerei ☐   [1]

4 You need to visit someone in hospital. Which sign should you follow?

A Verkehrsamt ☐   C Parkanlage ☐

B Krankenhaus ☐   D Stadion ☐   [1]

5 You pass a job centre and see the following notice in the window.

What job is being offered?   [1]

> **Wir suchen Kellner**
> **(☎) 01222/845678**

A   B   C   D

6 What job is being offered?

Ihre Chance   Ich suche einen Elektriker
(☎) 01222/876456

A  **B** 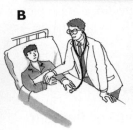 **C**  **D**

[1]

7 Sie gehen essen. Hier ist die Speisekarte.

—— City Grill ——

Fleischgerichte

Frikadelle	€ 2.00
Bratwurst	€ 2.50
Hamburger	€ 3.00
½ Hähnchen vom Grill	€ 4.00
Schnitzel	€ 4.50

Beilagen

Nudelsalat	€ 2.00
Pommes frites Portion	€ 2.00
Frischer Gurkensalat	€ 2.50

Getränke

Cola	0,3 L Dose	€ 0.90
Limo	0,3 L Dose	€ 0.90
Orangensaft		
	0,3 L Dose	€ 1.00
Mineralwasser		
	0,3 L Dose	€ 0.90
Tasse Kaffee		€ 1.80
Tasse Tee		€ 1.80

Bitte nicht rauchen!

Richtig oder falsch? Kreuzen Sie die richtigen Sätze an.

i) Eine  kostet € 1.80. ☐

ii) Eine  kostet € 2.50. ☐

iii) Ein 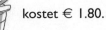 kostet € 3.80. ☐

iv) Eine kostet € 0.90. ☐

v) Die Speisekarte hat keine warmen Getränke. ☐   [5]

8 Was heißt „Bitte nicht rauchen!"?
Kreuzen Sie die richtige Antwort an.

A ☐ **C** ☐

B ☐ **D** ☐

[1]

9 Lesen Sie die Postkarte.

Freitag

Hallo!

Ich sitze hier im Freibad. Ich spiele jeden Tag Fußball mit den Leuten auf dem Campingplatz. Abends spielen wir meistens Tischtennis oder hören Musik.

Übermorgen müssen wir leider schon nach Hause zurück, denn Georg muss wieder arbeiten. Er ist Busfahrer in der Stadt.

Tschüss,
Gerd

Kreuzen Sie die richtige Antworten an.

i) Wo übernachtet Gerd?

A ☐   **B** ☐   **C** ☐   **D** ☐

[1]

ii) Wo schreibt Gerd seine Postkarte?

A ☐   **B** ☐   **C** ☐   **D** ☐

[1]

iii) Was spielt er jeden Tag mit seinen Freunden?
Kreuzen Sie **2** Kästchen an.

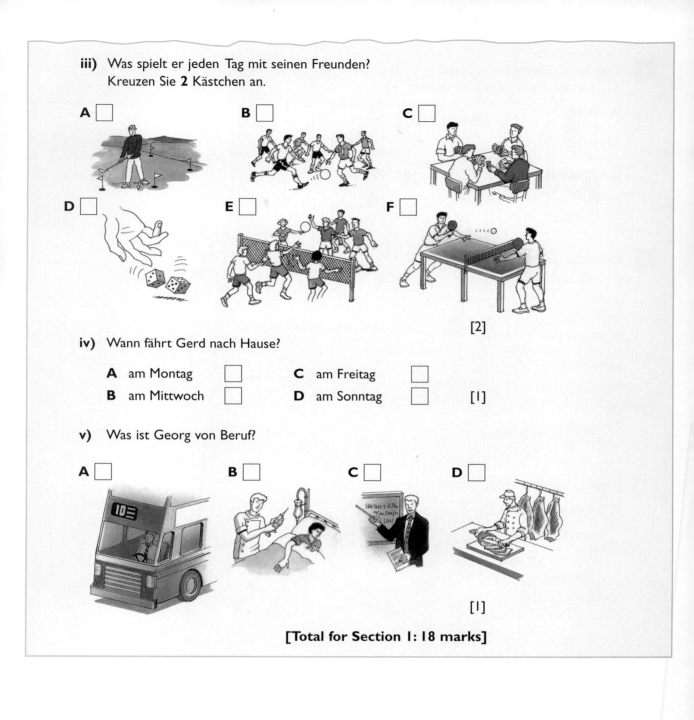

A ☐

B ☐

C ☐

D ☐

E ☐

F ☐

[2]

iv) Wann fährt Gerd nach Hause?

A am Montag ☐   **C** am Freitag ☐

B am Mittwoch ☐   **D** am Sonntag ☐   [1]

v) Was ist Georg von Beruf?

A ☐   **B** ☐   **C** ☐   **D** ☐

[1]

[Total for Section 1: 18 marks]

I Lesen Sie die Anzeigen.

FOUNDATION + HIGHER

A *Freizeitzentrum*
sucht Jugendliche(n)
zur Aushilfe im Kindergarten

B Warenhaus sucht
Jugendliche
zur Ausbildung in der
Musikabteilung

C   Blumen Kohl
Wir suchen Verkäufer(in)
Anfang September

D Haben Sie schon an der
Kasse gearbeitet? Ihr
Spar Supermarkt
stellt zum 1. Sept.
neue Mitarbeiter ein.

E   Elektro Statik –
Ihr Elektrofachgeschäft
im Citycenter
sucht 2 Auszubildende
für die Werkstatt

F   Fotografie als Beruf?
Besuchen Sie uns bei
Foto Brell
Am Hagedornweg 30

G   Esso an der Ubierstraße
braucht Tankwart ab sofort.
Kommen Sie vorbei!

Wo könnten die folgenden Leute arbeiten?

i)   Angela ist Hobbygärtnerin.   ☐

ii)   Thilo macht gern Aufnahmen.   ☐

iii) Susi spielt gern mit Kindern.   ☐

iv)   Peter mag Sachen reparieren.   ☐

v)   Linda hört gern Popmusik.   ☐

[5]

Düsseldorf, den 1. Februar

Hallo Frances, Hallo Michael!

Ich habe mich sehr über euren Brief gefreut. Vielen Dank für die Fotos von eurer Familie im Winterurlaub. Das Wetter hier war über die Feiertage nicht so toll wie bei euch – meist nass, kalt und neblig.

Ich muss bald wählen, was ich in der Oberstufe machen möchte, aber ich weiß noch nicht ganz, was ich für einen Beruf später machen soll. Vielleicht mache ich etwas mit Tieren, aber ich bin in Biologie ziemlich schlecht. Meine Eltern würden das ganz gut finden, glaube ich. Sie meinen, dass viel zu viele junge Leute den ganzen Tag am Computer sitzen. Sie sind mehr für die frische Luft, lange Spaziergänge, usw.

Mein Freund Dirk macht jetzt sein Abitur. Als Hauptfächer macht er Naturwissenschaften, und dazu lernt er Englisch und Mathe. Wenn alles gut geht, möchte er im kommenden Jahr sein Biostudium anfangen. Er freut sich schon darauf. Ich glaube, wir haben beide eine große Liebe für Tiere.

Hoffentlich läuft für euch beide alles klar in der Schule. Ihr habt wohl auch bald Prüfungen, nicht wahr?

Viele Grüße

Tschüss,

Ingrid

Wählen Sie die Antwort aus, die am besten passt. Füllen Sie die Lücken aus!

i) Frances und Michael sind Ingrids _____.
   Schulkameraden   Brieffreunde   Nachbarn

ii) Frances und Michael waren _____ im Urlaub.
   im Sommer   über Weihnachten   zu Ostern

iii) Ingrid _____, was sie beruflich machen will.
   weiß   ist sicher   hat keine Idee

iv) Ingrid _____.
   ist nicht so gut in Bio   ist sehr gut in Bio   findet Bio leicht

v) Ingrids Eltern _____ Computer.
   interessieren sich sehr für   arbeiten gern am   sind gegen

vi) Dirk möchte gern _____.
   weiterlernen   gleich mit Tieren arbeiten
   ein Arbeitspraktikum machen   [6]

[Total for Section 2: 11 marks]

I   Lesen Sie den folgenden Artikel.

WAS WILLST DU BERUFLICH MACHEN?

Mehr als 70 Prozent der Jugendlichen in der Bundesrepublik träumen von einem „richtig tollen Job". So heißt es in einer Umfrage. Sie zeigte auch, wie schnell die Träume sich ändern. Vor gar nicht langer Zeit wollten alle jungen Männer am liebsten als Förster im Freien arbeiten. Heute möchten sie Naturwissenschaftler werden (25%), mit Computern arbeiten (10%) oder als Manager arbeiten (9%). Die jungen Frauen ziehen es vor, als Künstlerin (15%), Managerin in einem Hotel (10%) oder als Fotomodell (7%) ihr Geld zu verdienen.

Eine große Überraschung war es, dass 85% von allen, die einen Beruf haben, mit ihrer Arbeit zufrieden sind! Ihren absoluten Traumberuf haben 12% der Männer und 5% der Frauen – oder so sagen sie.

Und wie möchten die meisten Leute arbeiten? Für viele ist es wichtig, dass sie den sichersten Arbeitgeber haben. Und wer soll das sein? Der Staat, natürlich.

Wann und wie lange Leute arbeiten möchten, steht auch fest: rund die Hälfte der Befragten sind gegen weniger Wochenstunden. Aber 75% wollen Teilzeitarbeit und flexible Arbeitszeiten. Und 90% wünschen sich mehr Urlaub!

Richtig oder falsch? Kreuzen Sie die richtigen Antworten an!

a) Die meisten jungen Leute haben einen Traumberuf. ☐

b) Der beliebteste Traumberuf von Männern bleibt unverändert. ☐

c) Ohne Traumberuf wird man am Arbeitsplatz nicht glücklich. ☐

d) Es gibt mehr Männer mit Traumberuf als Frauen. ☐

e) Die meisten Leute suchen Sicherheit bei der Arbeitsstelle. ☐

f) Die meisten Leute wollen keine feste Arbeitszeiten. ☐

[6]

Lesen Sie die folgende Broschüre aus dem Verkehrsamt in Bonn.

Herzlich Willkommen, liebe Besucher!

Genießen Sie einige schöne Ausflüge in der Bonner Gegend.

Das Siebengebirge (A) ist das älteste Naturschutzgebiet Europas. Den Gipfel des berühmten Berges **„Drachenfels" (B)**, erreicht man zu Fuß, per Bergbahn oder per Pferd.

Oben auf dem **Petersberg (C)**, steht ein Gasthaus mit einem herrlichen Ausblick, während unten am Rhein das pittoreske Weinstädtchen und Touristenparadies **Königswinter** (D) liegt.

In Rhöndorf können Sie eine Ausstellung über das Leben Konrad Adenauers besuchen. Das ehemalige **Wohnhaus (E)** des ersten Bundeskanzlers ist heute ein Museum.

Auf dem **Michaelsberg (F)** kann man tolle Wanderungen und Ausflüge im Forst machen.

Wie wäre es mit einem Spaziergang im Park des **Schlosses Augustusburg (G)** in Brühl? Auch ältere Leute können diese herrlichen Gärten aus dem Jahr 1725 sehen, ohne weit gehen zu müssen.

Ganz in der Nähe gibt es das Freizeit- und Abenteuerparadies **„Phantasialand" (H)** in Brühl. Dort findet man Unterhaltung und Spaß für Erwachsene genauso wie für Kinder.

Auch nicht weit von Bonn liegt die Stadt **Hennef (J)**, in deren engen Straßen man schöne, mittelalterliche Fachwerkhäuser und auch gemütliche, historische Gaststätten finden kann.

Wir wünschen Ihnen viel Vergnügen.

Ihre

STADT BONN

Finden Sie für jede Person in einer Familie ein passendes Ausflugsziel und schreiben Sie den Buchstaben.

a) Die Eltern wollen eine Weinprobe machen. ☐

b) Die Mutter möchte gern etwas Historisches sehen, aber auch zu Mittag essen gehen. ☐

c) Die kleinen Kinder wollen viel Spaß haben. ☐

d) Der Opa möchte beim Mittagessen eine schöne Aussicht genießen. ☐

e) Der älterer Bruder studiert die Geschichte der Bundesrepublik. ☐

f) Die Oma kann nicht weit laufen, möchte aber etwas Schönes sehen. ☐

[6]

3 *Lesen Sie das folgende Stück über die Schule in Deutschland. Jürgen freut sich auf den Sommer.*
Read the following passage about school in Germany. Jürgen is looking forward to the summer.

Nach den Osterferien gibt es viel mehr Sport bei uns in der Schule, was mir natürlich sehr gefällt.

In den Turnstunden gehen wir im Sommer meistens auf den Schulhof oder auf die Spielwiese, wenn es geht. Das macht uns allen mehr Spaß als immer in der Halle auf den Geräten zu turnen. Jemand hatte die Idee, einige Tennisplätze bei uns an der Schule anzulegen, aber es soll sehr teuer sein, und es können immer nur so wenig Leute auf einmal spielen. Ich glaube, es lohnt sich nicht.

Volleyball ist in meiner Klasse der Lieblingssport, und ein paar von uns organisieren im Juni ein Turnier für alle zehnten Klassen an unserer Schule. Hoffentlich gewinnt unsere Klasse!

Wir haben auch eine Arbeitsgemeinschaft für Rudern und ab der neunten Klasse darf man auf dem Rhein rudern. Wir leihen die Boote vom Ruderverein in der Stadt, und es kommt immer jemand vom Verein, der mit uns das Training macht. Dieses Jahr bereiten wir eine längere Fahrt vor, denn in den Sommerferien wollen wir eine Moseltour machen. Klasse! Darauf freue ich mich besonders.

In den nächsten Wochen schreiben wir in einigen Fächern Klausuren, und danach bekommen wir unsere Zeugnisse. Manche aus meiner Klasse haben Angst vor den Klassenarbeiten, aber ich glaube, es sind meistens nur die faulen Schüler. Ich denke, wenn man einigermaßen gut gearbeitet hat, sollte man die Prüfungen bestehen. Außerdem sind meine Eltern sehr vernünftig und verlangen immer nur, dass ich mein Bestes tue. Es gibt einen Elternabend im Juli, aber ich schaffe die Versetzung in die Oberstufe ohne Probleme. Leider glaubt meine Freundin Beate schon, dass sie sitzenbleiben wird.

Der Höhepunkt unseres Sommers ist das Schulfest im Juli mit der Disko abends in der Aula und draußen auf dem Schulhof. Es gibt Würstchen vom Grill, verschiedene Salate, mehrere Brotsorten und genug zu trinken, versteht sich! Normalerweise macht das einen Riesenspaß.

Kreuzen Sie die richtigen Sätze an.

a) In den Osterferien treibt man viel Sport in der Schule. ☐

b) Jürgen interessiert sich sehr viel für Sport. ☐

c) Das Volleyballturnier ist für alle Klassen. ☐

d) Der Wassersport ist nur für die jüngeren Schüler. ☐

e) Im Sommer macht Jürgen eine Moselfahrt. ☐

f) Jürgen hat keine Lust, Klassenarbeiten zu schreiben. ☐

g) Jürgen fürchtet, dass Beate sitzenbleibt. ☐

h) Jürgen findet das Klassenfest toll. ☐

i) Die Disko läuft den ganzen Tag. ☐

j) Es gibt immer genug zu essen und zu trinken. ☐ [10]

[Total for Section 3: 22 marks]

You will find the answers and examiner's comments on pages 173–5.

UNIT 17: EXAM PRACTICE
WRITING

How to overcome problems

As in the Speaking Test you have the great advantage of being able to play to your particular strengths, and to choose what you write to a great extent. Even when the topic is specified, along with certain details which you must include in your writing, you can express yourself as you wish. This is where you must exercise strong control over the language you use. You have to balance what you would like to say but feel unable to cope with structurally, against what you are able to say in German, which may be less adventurous. With regular practice of the Higher Level skills shown to you in this book, you should be able to increase what you can write with confidence.

☀ Problems and solutions

Problem 1
Understanding the question.

Solution
Make sure you are familiar with the requirements of the paper set by your exam board. The paper will follow a similar pattern each year, but at Higher Level you need to understand the whole range of questions which could be asked of you, not simply those which were set last year.

Problem 2
Deciding what you want to write.

Solution
Don't write a piece of English and then try to translate it. This will always cause you major problems. Instead, allow yourself time to plan, and write your piece once only. This is better than setting off in a rush and making a lot of mistakes and crossings out, hoping that you will have time to make a neater copy before the exam is over. If you are writing a letter which includes five major points, you will need to plan seven paragraphs in order to include the introduction and conclusion.

Try to work in German immediately. Write down the phrases you want to include alongside the paragraph number, according to what is required. Adverb phrases of time, manner and place make a good list, along with plenty of familiar words to reassure yourself at this early stage.

Problem 3

Knowing how much to write.

Solution

Some boards specify the length of what you are to write, in which case you must obviously take note of the guidelines. As a general rule, however, the letter required of you is usually between 80 and 100 words long, whereas the narrative piece is more likely to be between 130 and 150 words long. You shouldn't worry too much about writing up to ten words over the 'limit', but you should realise that you may lose marks for not reaching the required length. This may be because you therefore fail to mention some of the points you should. Alternatively, you may simply not be able to score sufficient marks if your work is too brief.

Problem 4

Producing work that is accurate.

Solution

'Check your work' is what all teachers will say to you before you give it in, but if you have made mistakes in the first place, how are you going to recognise them when you re-read your work? Use the following list of specific checks to highlight the most obvious pitfalls.

1   Make sure that *ich* is followed by a verb with an -*e* ending, and that *er* and *sie* and a person's name in the singular are followed by verbs that end in -*t* in the present tense. Verbs following *Sie* (or with a small s for 'they') will look like the infinitive and end in -*n* or -*en*.

2   Perfect tenses, of which you will have plenty in the Higher Level writing, must have two parts to the verb: the first is a part of *haben* or *sein* and the second is the past participle. A common mistake is to follow the subject with the past participle alone, such as *ich in die Stadt gegangen* or *ich gegangen in die Stadt* instead of *ich bin in die Stadt gegangen*.

3   Remind yourself of ten common verbs which take *sein* and try to use at least five of them in your piece of writing.

4   The adjectival agreement as described in earlier units can be quite complicated, but remind yourself of the 'eeeasiest' one of all, and use feminine nouns in the subject and object cases where possible.

Problem 5

Omitting a specified task and forfeiting the marks attached to it.

Solution

There must be no mistake here, as marks cannot be awarded for what is missing, no matter how brilliant the rest may be. Tick off on the exam paper the necessary items as you complete each one. Make a point of double-checking that you include them in any planning you do.

▰ Different kinds of question ▰

Questions vary according to the exam board you use, but they fall into a number of common types:

☀ Foundation Level questions

- The first question is usually a list of single words or phrases, and is identified with the F and G grades. This can vary from items you need for travelling, to a list of shopping for a picnic. There is some leeway on spelling and it is advisable not to use more than one or two words which are identical to English, such as *Butter*, *Anorak*, *Pullover*, etc.

- The second question is usually some sort of message or a postcard, with five tasks to fulfil in 30–40 words. The tasks are set either in German or by pictures, or both. You should aim to write in simple sentences. One of the tasks may require the use of a past or future tense. Messages are either left on the phone or by somebody calling by. Learn the two appropriate phrases to begin each of these eventualities:
  Herr Schmidt hat angerufen. Er möchte…
  Julia ist heute nachmittag vorbeigekommen. Sie sagt,…

- The third task – aimed at D and C grades – will probably be a letter, but may be an article, for which you may write up to 100 words. You are sometimes given a written stimulus, for example, a letter to which you have to respond. You will certainly need to use a range of past, present and future tenses in answering this sort of question.

☀ Higher Level questions

- The first question at Higher Level is the same as the last question at Foundation. This overlap in the two levels is aimed at candidates working in the area of Grades C and D.

- The second question will be a longer narrative, an article, report or sometimes another letter. The question will be in German and there may be a stimulus in German to help you, or even a set of pictures. The question is aimed at the three highest grades: B, A, and A*. As far as the language goes, accuracy is essential to get into this range of marks, but you are also expected to produce a sensible piece of writing which takes into account the stimulus given.

☀ Letters

Always begin with the date, thus: *Norwich, den 27. Mai.*

Formal
(To a youth hostel, hotel, camp-site, tourist office, etc. Also when writing to the parents of your penfriend.)

- Use *Sie* consistently throughout. Don't forget that the adjective is *Ihr*.

- Begin with *Sehr geehrter Herr Braun, Sehr geehrte Frau Braun*, if you know the name of the person, or *Sehr geehrte Herren*, if you don't.

- Finish with *Hochachtungsvoll* for a simple formal letter, or *Mit freundlichem Gruß*, if you know the person.

Informal
(To your penfriend, etc.)

- Use *du* and *dein* throughout the letter, or *ihr* and *euch* if you are referring to more than one member of the family.

- Begin with *Liebe Ingrid* or *Lieber Klaus*. The use of a exclamation mark is now largely outmoded.

- You can end with *Herzliche Grüße/Schöne Grüße* or similar and then *Dein* or *Deine* before your name.

☀ Articles

Sometimes you are asked to write an article for a German exchange school's magazine or similar. Once again, you are likely to be set certain tasks to fulfil within the article, or you may be given a written stimulus. You are more likely to stick to one topic within an article, rather than covering several as in a letter. If you can use both 1st person singular and plural – *ich* and *wir* – your writing may become less repetitive.

☀ Accounts

The longest piece of writing at this level is up to 150 words in length. Daunting as this may seem at first, if tackled methodically you can soon achieve this length. You may even find yourself having to trim back a little when you have finished, if your account runs to more than 160 words.

The account is always set in the past, but if it is possible to include a future tense, perhaps in some direct speech, this is all the better. In an account based on six pictures, you simply need to divide the narrative into six parts and write two to three sentences about each picture. Even if the stimulus is more general, you still need to work out how to break down the narrative into paragraphs of a manageable length. By doing so, you can be certain not to omit a major part of the account.

Higher Level performance

Using a variety of tenses

- Do remember that you must show your ability to use the past, present and future tenses, and you must be able to express opinions in order to attain a Grade C. Here is a quick reminder of when to use which tense:

  - **Perfect** for actions:
    ich bin gegangen/ich habe gekauft

  - **Imperfect** for weather, circumstances and feelings:
    Es war herrliches Wetter/wir waren alle müde/ich freute mich, dass...

  - **Imperfect** for modal verbs:
    Wir wollten/ich musste/wir sollten/er durfte nicht, etc.

  - Try having a **pluperfect** up your sleeve just to impress the examiner:
    Es war ein schöner Tag gewesen.
    Ich hatte den Film schon gesehen.

  - **Present** – usually for use in a letter not in the narrative. Watch all those common irregular verbs in the 3rd person:
    liest/fährt/trifft/sieht, etc.

  - **Future** – with *werden, wollen, vorhaben, planen, hoffen*.

Using longer and fuller sentences

- Don't forget that your work takes on the appearance of the Grade A candidate you want to be when you express yourself in longer sentences, rather than in the style of your first simple sentences. Use the conjunctions you have learned, in order to achieve double the sentence with little extra effort.

- Remember that coordinating conjunctions (*und, denn* and *aber*) are easier than all the others, which are subordinating and force you to change the word order:
    Wir mussten lange warten, denn mein Vater hatte seinen Pass vergessen.
    Ich bin schnell nach Hause gegangen, weil ich die Tasche holen wollte.

- *Um ... zu* can replace a clause but still has the effect of lengthening your sentence:
    Ich bin nach Hause gegangen, um die Tasche zu holen.

- Use the relative clause to add extra detail in a natural way:
    Mein Bruder hat eine CD gekauft, die im Sonderangebot war.

- Prepare to express opinions in a variety of ways:
    Ich fand die Platte nicht besonders gut.
    Meiner Meinung nach war die Musik furchtbar.

- Use adjectives and adjectival phrases:
    Der Mann mit dem doofen Hut ist mein Onkel.

- Use adverbs and adverbial phrases:
    *Ich bin erst am späten Nachmittag mit dem Fahrrad in die
        Schule gekommen.*

- Fill in the background details of weather and circumstance:
    Ich fand meine Oma zu Hause, weil das Wetter so schlecht war.

Making use of any German which is on the question paper

- It is virtually certain that you will not be able to copy a sentence from the question paper and use it in your answer, but there may well be words and even phrases which you can turn to your advantage. Make sure you have understood them correctly.

- If there are direct questions or instructions, you may simply be able to rephrase for your purposes. For example, if the instruction is:
    Erzählen Sie, was Sie in den Osterferien gemacht haben.

    you could base your answer on:
    In den Osterferien habe ich ... gemacht.

- If the stimulus is an advertisement for a product, service or a job, you may be able to extract specific words which will help. For example, a job advert may contain the words *Ihr Gehalt* or *€10.00 pro Stunde.*

████ **Questions to try** ████

The writing examination is marked out of 50. A likely mark scheme is shown in brackets at the end of each question.

Foundation candidates complete **Section 1** (30 marks) and **Section 2** (20 marks).
Time allowed: 40 minutes.
Higher candidates complete **Section 2** (20 marks) and **Section 3** (30 marks).
Time allowed: 60 minutes.

SECTION 1   FOUNDATION   30 marks

FOUNDATION

1 You are packing to go on holiday. Write a list of **8** items to take with you.

Example ———— *zahnpasta* ————

1 _____

2 _____

3 _____

4 _____

5 _____

6 _____

7 _____

8 _____

[8]

2 Fill the gaps in German with a phrase suggested by the picture.

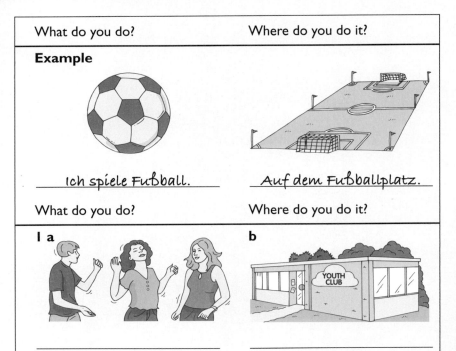

What do you do?	Where do you do it?
Example	
Ich spiele Fußball.	_Auf dem Fußballplatz._
What do you do?	Where do you do it?
1 a	**b**
	YOUTH CLUB
_____	_____

2 a

b

_____

3 a

b

_____   _____

[Communication: 6 marks]
[Accuracy: 3 marks]
[Total: 9 marks]

3 Write a postcard to a friend in Austria, saying what you are doing on holiday. Write about 40 words in complete sentences.

Mention the following:

- Weather
- Activity
- Family
- Cinema
- Meals
- Shopping

[Communication: 6 marks]
[Accuracy: 7 marks]
[Total: 13 marks]

[Total for Section 1: 30 marks]

SECTION 2   FOUNDATION AND HIGHER   20 marks

*Answer **either** Question 1 **or** Question 2.*

Schreiben Sie 90–100 Wörter auf Deutsch.

1 Schreiben Sie einen Brief zum Thema Schule an einen Brieffreund/
eine Brieffreundin.

Erwähnen Sie folgendes:

- Fächer
- Sport
- Letzte Woche (Aktivitäten, mit wem?)
- Zukunftspläne (Fächer? Studieren?)   [20]

2 Schreiben Sie eine E-mail an einen Brieffreund/eine Brieffreundin.

Erwähnen Sie folgendes:

- Ihr Arbeitsplatz (wo arbeiten Sie? Firma?)
- Aufgaben (was machen Sie?)
- Wie viel Geld Sie verdienen
- Was Sie mit dem Geld machen (Urlaub? Geschenke? Sparen?)
- 2 Vorteile oder Nachteile (gute Arbeit/schlechte Arbeit?)   [20]

Mark scheme for Section 2
Communication: 10 marks
Quality of language: 6 marks
Accuracy: 4 marks

[Total for Section 2: 20 marks]

[Total for Foundation and Higher Paper: 50 marks]

SECTION 3   HIGHER   20 marks

*Answer **either** Question 1 **or** Question 2.*

Schreiben Sie 140–50 Wörter auf Deutsch.

1 Schreiben Sie einen Aufsatz mit dem Titel ‚Ein katastrophaler Urlaub‘.

Erwähnen Sie folgende Punkte:

- Wo haben Sie Urlaub gemacht, und warum?
- Wie war das Hotel/die Jugendherberge/die Pension?
- Ist etwas Besonderes passiert?
- Wie war das Wetter?
- Welche Ausflüge haben Sie gemacht?   [30]

2 Sie haben einen Verkehrsunfall gesehen. Schreiben Sie einen Bericht für die Polizei. Erklären Sie, was Sie gesehen haben und wie der Unfall passiert ist.

(This is a very open question and can be off-putting if you have not prepared an answer The 'traffic accident' is a GCSE standard, so make sure you have a 'plot' ready.)

[30]

[Total for Section 3: 30 marks]

[Total for Higher Paper: 50 marks]

You will find sample answers and examiner's comments on pages 175–8.

UNIT 18: FURTHER GRAMMAR

▰ Verbs ▰

The form of the verb in German is determined by the subject, or 'person' doing the verb. The verb is therefore often referred to as being in the 1st, 2nd or 3rd 'person'.

- The **1st** person is used when the person speaking is doing the verb:
  ich in the singular
  wir in the plural

- The **2nd** person of the verb is the 'you' form:
  du for family and friends in the singular
  ihr for family and friends in the plural
  Sie for polite or formal use, whether singular or plural

- The **3rd** person is used for all other people or things:
  Georg, Charlotte, er, sie, es (he/she/it) and *man* (one) are singular.
  Katherine und Anne, die Leute and *sie* (they) are plural.

Verb tables are usually written in the following form:

Singular	Plural
ich	wir
du	ihr
Sie	Sie
er/sie/es/man	sie

NOTE: Because the *Sie* form is used in both singular and plural, it is included in both lists even though the form is identical.

☼ Impersonal verbs

- These are verbs used in certain fixed expressions, in the 3rd person singular with *es*:

  - *geben*
Es gibt	There is/are
Es gab	There was/were
    (Notice that this form covers both singular and plural.)
  - *gelingen*
    Es ist mir gelungen, ... *zu* + infinitive:
    Es ist uns gelungen, Konzertkarten für heute abend zu bekommen.
        We succeeded in getting concert tickets for this evening.
  - *stimmen*
    Es stimmt (nicht).   That's (not) true./That's (not) right.
  - *gefallen*
    Es gefällt mir.   I like it.
    Es gefiel ihr nicht.   She didn't like it.
  - **Weather expressions**
    Es friert.
    Es regnet.
    Es schneit.

☼ The conditional

- This is much more a matter of recognition than of use, although you will, of course, impress the examiner if you can introduce a conditional sentence into your spoken or written work.

- If the conditional sentence expresses something which is more or less certain, then you will see the present and future indicative tenses used:
  *Wenn es **regnet**, **wird** die Straße naß.*
  *Wenn er **kommt**, dann **gehe** ich sofort.*
  *Wenn du Glück **hast**, **kommt** er nicht.*

- If the condition is less likely to be fulfilled, then you will encounter subjunctives, usually the imperfect tenses of *haben, sein* or *werden*, but sometimes the modal verbs in the imperfect subjunctive:
  *Wenn ich viel Geld **hätte**, **würde** ich einen Porsche kaufen.*
  *Ich **könnte** das auch machen, wenn ich **müßte**.*

- Here are some imperfect subjunctive forms which you may well see:

sein	*ich wäre*	I would be
haben	*ich hätte*	I would have
werden	*ich würde*	I would + any infinitive
MODALS		
dürfen	*ich dürfte*	I would be allowed to
können	*ich könnte*	I could
mögen	*ich möchte*	I would like to
müssen	*ich müßte*	I would have to
sollen	*ich sollte*	I should, ought to
wollen	*ich wollte*	I wanted

☼ The passive

- At Higher Level, you need to recognise the passive form in the present, imperfect and perfect tenses. It is formed by using the appropriate tense of *werden* with the past participle:

  - **Present**
    Unser Wagen wird heute repariert.　　Our car is being repaired today.

  - **Imperfect**
    Unser Wagen wurde gestern repariert.　　Our car was repaired yesterday.

  - **Perfect**
    Unser Wagen ist schon repariert worden.　　Our car has been repaired already.

- You should be able to use the *man* form in place of the passive at Higher Level:
  Man schenkt uns oft so 'was.　　We are often given things like that.
  Man rief ihn gestern abend an.　　He was telephoned last night.
  Man hat ihnen das geschenkt.　　They were given it.

HIGHER UNDERSTANDING

☼ The subjunctive _____

- Your use of this form of the verb need only be very limited. You should be able to use *möchte* and *könnte* in these common ways:
   Ich möchte ein Eis.
   Möchten Sie/Möchtest du ...?
   Ich könnte in die Stadt gehen.
   Könnten Sie/Könntest du mitkommen?

HIGHER UNDERSTANDING

- You should also be able to **recognise** the imperfect subjunctive of *sein*, *haben* and *werden* in the conditional, as described on page 130.

☼ The infinitive _____

- The uses of the infinitive are many, but all are easily understood:

  - **After modals**
     Du sollst es lernen.
     Ich möchte dahin gehen.
     Könntest du mir dein Rad leihen?

  - **After *gehen***
     Ich gehe heute schwimmen.
     Sie gingen heute vormittag einkaufen.
     Er ist angeln gegangen.

  - **After *um ... zu***
     Ich gehe in die Stadt, um eine Hose zu kaufen.

  - **After verbs requiring *zu***
     Es beginnt zu regnen.
     Ich versuche das Problem zu lösen.

HIGHER

- At Higher Level, you should also be able to use *lassen* with an infinitive to imply 'having something done':
   Ich lasse mir die Haare schneiden.
   Meine Mutter läßt das Auto reparieren.

Nouns

☼ Gender

- All German nouns are either masculine, feminine or neuter. It is essential that you adopt the habit of writing down and learning the gender of nouns as you meet them. If you can't remember the gender, you won't be able to use the word effectively in either your speaking or writing. Below are some general rules on gender which may help you.

- Masculine words – *der/ein*

    - Male people and animals
      der Manager   manager
      der Löwe   lion

    - Days, months, seasons
      der Samstag
      der Juli
      der Herbst

    - Compass points/most types of weather
      der Süden/im Süden
      der Hagel
      der Regen

    - Nouns ending in:
-ig	*der Pfennig*	penny
-ling	*der Lehrling*	apprentice
-ant	*der Protestant*	protestant (except ***das** Restaurant*)
-er	*der Sprecher*	speaker
-ismus	*der Marxismus*	marxism
-or	*der Rektor*	headteacher, principal

- Feminine words – *die/eine*

    - Female people and animals
      die Tante   aunt
      die Löwin   lioness

    - Names of numbers
      die Eins
      eine Million

    - Nouns ending in:
-ion	*die Information*	information
-anz	*die Substanz*	substance
-enz	*die Lizenz*	licence
-ie	*die Kopie*	copy
-ik	*die Republik*	republic
-ur	*die Figur*	figure
-age	*die Garage*	garage
-ette	*die Diskette*	floppy disk

■ Neuter words – *das/ein*

- Young people and animals
das Kind	child
das Mädchen	girl
das Baby	baby
das Lamm	lamb

- Measurements
das Meter	meter
das Kilo	kilogramme
das Liter	litre

- Letters of the alphabet
  ein großes S a capital S (*London wird mit großem L geschrieben.*)

- Colours
das Grün	green

- Languages
das Englisch	English

- Words 'borrowed' from other languages
das Café	café
das Hotel	hotel
das Mikrofon	microphone

- Nouns ending in:
-um	das Wachstum	growth (except *der Reichtum* [riches] and *der Irrtum* [error])
-ment	*das Argument*	argument, reason
-ett	*das Bukett*	bouquet
-icht	*das Gewicht*	weight

☀ Compound nouns

■ In compound nouns, it is always the last part of the word that determines the gender and plural form of the noun:
der Stundenplan	timetable
die Bushaltestelle	bus-stop
das Schwimmbad	swimming pool

☀ Plural nouns

■ Here are some simple guidelines as to how nouns form their plurals.

- Masculine
  Most form their plural with an *-e*; on some an umlaut is added to the last vowel:
  Stadtplan → Stadtpläne

  If the noun ends in *-el*, *-en* or *-er*, it is usual for it to stay the same in the plural.

- **Feminine**
  Virtually all form their plural by adding -*n* or -*en*.
  Two common exceptions are:
    Mutter → Mütter
    Tochter → Töchter

- **Neuter**
  Most neuter nouns add an -*e* to form their plural.
  The other common plural form is an umlaut and -*er*:
    Blatt → Blätter

☼ Declension

- In the genitive singular of both masculine and neuter nouns, the noun adds an -*s* or an -*es*:

  - Words with two syllables or more add -*s*:
    das Auto meines Vaters

  - Words with one syllable add -*es*:
    der Titel des Buches

- All nouns add -*n* or -*en* in the dative plural:
    Sie spricht mit den zwei Kindern.

Number and time

The cardinal numbers

0	Null	11	elf	22	zweiundzwanzig
1	eins	12	zwölf	23	dreiundzwanzig
2	zwei	13	dreizehn	24	vierundzwanzig
3	drei	14	vierzehn	25	fünfundzwanzig
4	vier	15	fünfzehn	26	sechsundzwanzig
5	fünf	16	sechzehn	27	siebenundzwanzig
6	sechs	17	siebzehn	28	achtundzwanzig
7	sieben	18	achtzehn	29	neunundzwanzig
8	acht	19	neunzehn	30	dreißig
9	neun	20	zwanzig	31	einunddreißig
10	zehn	21	einundzwanzig	32	zweiunddreißig, usw.

100	hundert
1000	tausend
1,000,000	eine Million

Quantity
Notice that you do not need to translate the English 'of':

achtzig Liter Benzin	*80 litres of petrol*
vier Kilo Tomaten	*4 kilos of tomatoes*
drei Meter Seide	*3 metres of silk*

Dates and time
You will need to use ordinal numbers for dates:

(der) erste/(der) 1ste	fünfte
zweite	sechste
dritte	siebte
vierte	

Then *achte* as far as *neunzehnte* – all adding *-te*.
Then *zwanzigste*, *einundzwanzigste*, etc. – all adding *-ste*.
> *Heute ist der vierundzwanzigste Juni.* (*der 24ste Juni/der 24. Juni*)
> *Vati kommt erst am sechsundzwanzigsten Juli.*
> (*am 26sten Juli/am 26. Juli*)

Seit and *schon*
In German, you use the present tense with *seit* or *schon* to translate the idea of doing something for a length of time:

Ich lerne Deutsch seit	I have been learning German
zwei Jahren.	**for** two years.
Wir sind schon zwei Tage hier.	We have been here **for** two days.

Similarly, *seit* or *schon* used with the imperfect tense translates as 'had been ...'.

Prepositions and cases

■ **Prepositions which take the accusative case**

bis	gegen
durch	ohne
entlang	um
für	

Sie bleibt bis nächsten Dienstag.
Er lief durch die Stadt.
Er fuhr die Straße entlang*.
Ist das für meinen Bruder?
Wir spielten gegen die Mannschaft aus Düsseldorf.
Ohne deinen Kuli kannst du nichts schreiben.
Wir liefen um das Schulgebaüde.

* Note that *entlang* usually follows the noun.

■ **Prepositions which take the dative case**

aus	nach
außer	seit
bei	von
gegenüber	zu
mit	

Sie nimmt das Geld aus ihrer Tasche.
Niemand weiß es außer meinem Vetter.
Ich habe bei meinem Onkel gewohnt.
Das Haus steht gegenüber dem Kino.*
Sie fährt mit dem Zug.
Nach dem Mittagessen gehen wir nach Hause.
Seit dem Tod seines Hundes geht er kaum spazieren.
Er läuft von der Schule zu der Haltestelle.

* Also: *dem Kino gegenüber*. If *gegenüber* is used with a pronoun, the pronoun must come first: *Er stand mir gegenüber.*

■ **Prepositions which take either the accusative or dative**
These prepositions take either the accusative or dative, depending on whether you wish to show movement or position:

an	neben
auf	über
hinter	unter
in	zwischen

Accusative

Sie fuhren ans (= an das) Meer.
Die Katze sprang auf den Stuhl.
Er lief hinter das Haus.

Dative

Sie saßen am (= an dem) Strand.
Die Katze sitzt auf dem Stuhl.
Der Wagen stand hinter dem Haus.

■ **Prepositions which take the genitive case**

> trotz
> während
> wegen

> *Trotz des Regens bleiben wir eine Weile im Garten.*
> *Während des Tages arbeiten wir zu Hause.*
> *Wegen des Verkehrs sind wir zu spät angekommen.*

Note that *wegen* is now frequently followed by the dative case: *wegen dem Verkehr, wegen dem Wetter*, etc.

■ **Contractions of preposition and article**
Certain prepositions combine with the definite article as follows:

> an dem → am
> an das → ans
> bei dem → im
> in dem → im
> in das → ins
> von dem → vom
> zu dem → zum
> zu der → zur

> *Ich laufe zur Haltestelle, fahre ins Dorf und kaufe die Wurst beim Metzger.*

■ **Use of *da(r)* with prepositions**
If you want to follow a preposition by the word 'it', you use the word *da* in front of the preposition (regardless of the gender of the word to which the pronoun 'it' refers). If the preposition begins with a vowel, add an *r*.

> *Ich nehme einen Kuli und schreibe **damit**.* (with it)
> *Dort ist dein Stuhl. Setz' dich **darauf**.* (on it)
> *Wir haben nur die eine Tasse, aber du darfst **daraus** trinken.* (out of it)

Word order in main clauses

■ In a main clause, the finite verb is always the 'second idea'. (The finite verb is the part of the verb which is governed directly by the subject; it is not the infinitive or the past participle.) That does not mean it is necessarily the second word, as the 'first idea' may be a phrase.

Subject	Verb	Rest of main clause
Er	kommt	um zehn Uhr nach Hause.
Meine Mutter	fährt	morgen mit ihrer Schwester nach Bonn.
Die Dame mit dem Hund	steht	neben meiner Tante.
Mein Bruder und ich	wollen	heute nicht einkaufen gehen.
Sie	müssen	den neuen Film unbedingt sehen.
Ich	hoffe,	morgen die neue CD zu kaufen.
Meine Freunde	sind	letzte Woche nach Berlin mitgefahren.
Wir	haben	die Hausaufgaben ganz leicht gefunden.
Adverb or adverb phrase	**Verb**	**Subject, then rest of clause**
Um zehn Uhr	kommt	er nach Hause.
Morgen	fährt	meine Mutter mit ihrer Schwester nach Bonn.
Neben meiner Tante	steht	die Dame mit dem Hund.
Heute	wollen	meine Bruder und ich nicht einkaufen gehen.
Den neuen Film	müssen	Sie unbedingt sehen.
Morgen	hoffe	ich, die neue CD zu kaufen.
Letzte Woche	sind	meine Freunde nach Berlin gefahren.
Die Hausaufgaben	haben	wir ganz leicht gefunden.

■ Watch out for the direct object appearing as the first idea for emphasis. It can sometimes be confusing:

Den Knochen hat der Hund schnell gefressen.

Common sense should dictate whether the dog ate the bone or the bone ate the dog! In this example, the masculine accusative is obvious, but it is not obvious with feminine and neuter nouns:

Ihre Tochter hat die Frau sofort mitgenommen.

You must decide from the context whether this means 'Your daughter took the woman with her straight away' or 'The woman took her daughter with her straight away'. On the other hand, *Das neue Auto fand Frau Braun ganz toll* can only mean one thing.

Verb tables

☀ Weak (regular) verbs

abholen	to fetch	gucken	to look	spielen	to play
abräumen	to clear away	heiraten	to marry	stecken	to put
abspülen	to wash up	hoffen	to hope	stellen	to put
anmachen	to switch on	hören	to hear	stimmen	to be correct
antworten	to answer	kaufen	to buy	suchen	to look for
arbeiten	to work	klingeln	to ring a bell	tanzen	to dance
aufhören	to stop	klopfen	to knock	teilen	to share
aufmachen	to open	kriegen	to get (coll.)	träumen	to dream
aufpassen	to pay attention	lachen	to laugh	turnen	to do gymnastics
aufwachen	to wake up	legen	to put	üben	to practise
ausmachen	to switch off	lernen	to learn	überraschen	to surprise
auspacken	to unpack	machen	to make	verdienen	to earn
sich beeilen	to hurry	meinen	to think, say	verkaufen	to sell
begrüßen	to greet	mieten	to rent, hire	vermieten	to rent out
besichtigen	to visit	nähen	to sew	versuchen	to try
bestellen	to order	öffnen	to open	vorbereiten	to prepare
besuchen	to visit	prüfen	to test, check	wählen	to choose
bezahlen	to pay	rauchen	to smoke	warten	to wait
brauchen	to need	regnen	to rain	wechseln	to change (money)
buchen	to book	reichen	to pass	wecken	to wake
danken	to thank	reisen	to travel	wiederholen	to repeat
decken	to lay (table)	reparieren	to repair	wohnen	to live
drücken	to press, push	sagen	to say	wünschen	to wish
einkaufen	to shop	sammeln	to collect	zahlen	to pay
einpacken	to pack up	schauen	to look, watch	zeichnen	to draw
fehlen	to be missing	schicken	to send	zeigen	to show
fragen	to ask	schmecken	to taste	zuhören	to listen
sich freuen	to be pleased	schneien	to snow		
glauben	to believe	segeln	to sail		

☀ Strong (irregular) verbs

Infinitive	Present (3rd person)	Imperfect (1st and 3rd person)	Perfect (*haben* or *sein** + past participle)	Meaning
anfangen	fängt an	fing an	angefangen	to begin
aufstehen	steht auf	stand auf	aufgestanden*	to get up
beginnen	beginnt	begann	begonnen	to begin
beißen	beißt	biss	gebissen	to bite
bekommen	bekommt	bekam	bekommen	to get, receive
beschließen	beschließt	beschloss	beschlossen	to decide
beschreiben	beschreibt	beschrieb	beschrieben	to describe
biegen	biegt	bog	gebogen	to bend
bieten	bietet	bot	geboten	to offer
bitten	bittet	bat	gebeten	to ask, request
bleiben	bleibt	blieb	geblieben*	to stay
brechen	bricht	brach	gebrochen	to break
brennen	brennt	brannte	gebrannt	to burn
bringen	bringt	brachte	gebracht	to bring
denken	denkt	dachte	gedacht	to think
dürfen	darf	durfte		to be allowed
einladen	lädt ein	lud ein	eingeladen	to invite
empfehlen	empfiehlt	empfahl	empfohlen	to recommend
erhalten	erhält	erhielt	erhalten	to receive
erkennen	erkennt	erkannte	erkannt	to recognise
essen	isst	aß	gegessen	to eat
fahren	fährt	fuhr	gefahren*	to travel
fallen	fällt	fiel	gefallen*	to fall
fangen	fängt	fing	gefangen	to catch
finden	findet	fand	gefunden	to find
fliegen	fliegt	flog	geflogen*	to fly
geben	gibt	gab	gegeben	to give
gefallen	gefällt	gefiel	gefallen	to please
gehen	geht	ging	gegangen*	to go
geschehen	geschieht	geschah	geschehen*	to happen
gewinnen	gewinnt	gewann	gewonnen	to win
haben	hat	hatte	gehabt	to have
halten	hält	hielt	gehalten	to hold
helfen	hilft	half	geholfen	to help
kennen	kennt	kannte	gekannt	to know
kommen	kommt	kam	gekommen*	to come
können	kann	konnte		to be able to, can

Infinitive	Present (3rd person)	Imperfect (1st and 3rd person)	Perfect (*haben* or *sein** + past participle)	Meaning
lassen	*läßt*	*ließ*	*gelassen*	to let, leave
laufen	*läuft*	*lief*	*gelaufen**	to run
leihen	*leiht*	*lieh*	*geliehen*	to lend
lesen	*liest*	*las*	*gelesen*	to read
liegen	*liegt*	*lag*	*gelegen*	to lie
mögen	*mag*	*mochte*		to like
müssen	*muss*	*musste*		to have to, must
nehmen	*nimmt*	*nahm*	*genommen*	to take
reißen	*reißt*	*riss*	*gerissen*	to tear
reiten	*reitet*	*ritt*	*geritten**	to ride (horse)
riechen	*riecht*	*roch*	*gerochen*	to smell
rufen	*ruft*	*rief*	*gerufen*	to call
scheinen	*scheint*	*schien*	*geschienen*	to shine
schießen	*schießt*	*schoss*	*geschossen*	to shoot
schlafen	*schläft*	*schlief*	*geschlafen*	to sleep
schlagen	*schlägt*	*schlug*	*geschlagen*	to hit
schließen	*schließt*	*schloss*	*geschlossen*	to close
schneiden	*schneidet*	*schnitt*	*geschnitten*	to cut
schreiben	*schreibt*	*schrieb*	*geschrieben*	to write
schreien	*schreit*	*schrie*	*geschrieen*	to shout, scream
schwimmen	*schwimmt*	*schwamm*	*geschwommen**	to swim
sehen	*sieht*	*sah*	*gesehen*	to see
sein	*ist*	*war*	*gewesen**	to be
singen	*singt*	*sang*	*gesungen*	to sing
sinken	*sinkt*	*sank*	*gesunken**	to sink
sitzen	*sitzt*	*saß*	*gesessen*	to sit
sollen	*soll*	*sollte*		should, ought to
sprechen	*spricht*	*sprach*	*gesprochen*	to speak
springen	*springt*	*sprang*	*geprungen**	to jump
stehen	*steht*	*stand*	*gestanden*	to stand
stehlen	*stiehlt*	*stahl*	*gestohlen*	to steal
sterben	*stirbt*	*starb*	*gestorben**	to die
tragen	*trägt*	*trug*	*getragen*	to wear, carry
treten	*tritt*	*trat*	*getreten**	to tread, step
trinken	*trinkt*	*trank*	*getrunken*	to drink
tun	*tut*	*tat*	*getan*	to do
verbringen	*verbringt*	*verbrachte*	*verbracht*	to spend
vergessen	*vergisst*	*vergaß*	*vergessen*	to forget

Infinitive	Present (3rd person)	Imperfect (1st and 3rd person)	Perfect (*haben* or *sein** + past participle)	Meaning
verlassen	*verläßt*	*verließ*	*verlassen*	to leave (place)
verlieren	*verliert*	*verlor*	*verloren*	to lose
verschwinden	*verschwindet*	*verschwand*	*verschwunden**	to disappear
versprechen	*verspricht*	*versprach*	*versprochen*	to promise
verstehen	*versteht*	*verstand*	*verstanden*	to understand
waschen	*wäscht*	*wusch*	*gewaschen*	to wash
werden	*wird*	*wurde*	*geworden**	to become
werfen	*wirft*	*warf*	*geworfen*	to throw
wissen	*weiß*	*wusste*	*gewusst*	to know
wollen	*will*	*wollte*	*gewollt*	to want
ziehen	*zieht*	*zog*	*gezogen*	to pull

* Verbs marked with an asterisk use *sein* to form the perfect and pluperfect tenses.

CHECK YOURSELF ANSWERS

UNIT 1: DIE SCHULE
1 What you need to know (page 2)

Q1

A Mein Lieblingsfach ist Geschichte.
B Ich bekomme gute Noten in Mathe.
C Wir turnen in der Turnhalle.
D Ich fahre jeden Tag mit dem Bus zur Schule.
E Jede Stunde dauert sechzig Minuten.

Comments

A Take care not to confuse *Geschichte* with *das Gesicht*.
B Don't be misled by *Noten*, meaning 'marks'. It also means 'musical notes'.
C German speakers use *turnen* for any sort of PE in the gym. Take care not to use *Gymnasium* for anything to do with sport.
D Remember the order of adverb phrases: Time, Manner, Place.
E Avoid *Jede Stunde dauert eine Stunde.*

Q2

A 2
B 6
C 3
D 7
E 9

Comments

Exam boards are making increasing use of visual materials, including standardised icons to represent many everyday objects and also feelings such as liking or disliking something. You need to familiarise yourself with the sort of visual material that is available. Most of it should be obvious, since it is widely used in language teaching books, but there may be subjects or items beyond your experience. Don't be afraid to ask your teacher what is meant.

2 Higher vocabulary (page 3)

Q1

A Mathe finde ich langweilig, aber ich bin sehr gut in Geschichte.
B Mein Bruder und ich kommen gewöhnlich mit dem Auto in die Schule, außer wenn es sehr schönes Wetter ist.
C In der Mittagspause treffe ich mich mit meiner Schwester in der Kantine.
D Im September möchte ich Musik, Englisch und Geschichte studieren.
E Ich möchte Ingenieur werden.

Comments

A Putting the word *Mathe* first adds emphasis. Remember to invert afterwards and put the verb next.
B *Außer wenn* is the sort of construction which will earn extra credit.
C The adverb phrase *In der Mittagspause* is first, so invert immediately afterwards.
D *Im* with months of the year.
E Remember to omit the indefinite article in German.

3 How the grammar works (page 5)

Q1

A Wie heißt deine/eure/Ihre Schwester?
B Ich bringe meinen Bruder mit.
C Das ist das Auto meiner Mutter.
D Das Mädchen geht mit seinem Freund/seiner Freundin spazieren.
E Haben Sie Ihre Taschen vergessen, Frau Wenzler?

Comments

A Use *eure* if you are talking to two friends as *ihr*, and *Ihre* if you are using the polite form *Sie* in a formal situation.
B Remember to add the *mit*. This translates the English 'with me'.
C *Meiner Mutter* is obviously feminine, although it refers to *das Auto*.
D This is a tricky one, but it comes up frequently. The German word for girl is *das Mädchen*, and therefore the possessive must be *sein*.

E You need the polite form *Sie* and *Ihr* when talking to this woman.

Q2

A She is my friend's sister.

B My friends are annoyed because I can't find our dog.

C Please take her bag with you and give it to her.

D The girls met their mothers in the department store.

Comments

A Take extra care where two people are involved. It may be confusing, but you need to be clear about the difference between my 'teacher's brother' and 'my brother's teacher'.

B Don't assume an automatic connection between a person mentioned and the possessive adjective which follows.

C Again, the formal *Sie* is likely to lead you astray with the *ihre* which follows, just as the *sie* in the second clause might lead you to believe that the bag has something to do with 'them'.

D Remember that *Mädchen* is a neuter word and that therefore *Die Mädchen* must be plural. Similarly, the umlaut on *Mütter* shows you that it is plural. Higher Level candidates are expected to know the plurals of common nouns.

UNIT 2: MEIN HAUS, MEIN ZIMMER

1 What you need to know (page 7)

Q1

A Ich wohne in einem Doppelhaus.

B Wir haben eine neue Küche.

C In meinem Zimmer habe ich einen Schreibtisch und einen Stuhl.

D Meine Eltern arbeiten im Garten.

E Wir haben ein Sofa und zwei Sessel im Wohnzimmer.

Comments

B Remember the feminine agreements are 'eeeasy'.

C Remember to turn around the subject and verb after a phrase at the beginning of the sentence.

D Use the contraction *im* whenever possible.

2 Higher vocabulary (page 9)

Q1

A Ich finde mein Schlafzimmer sehr gemütlich.

B Unser Wohnzimmer ist sehr bequem, aber oft unordentlich.

C Ich verbringe viel Zeit in der Küche, wo wir auch meistens essen.

D Ich stehe normalerweise so gegen sieben Uhr auf.

E Ich gehe ins Esszimmer und frühstücke mit meinem Vater.

Comments

A It is easier to use the *ich finde* construction than *ich denke, dass*.

B *Bequem* refers to physical comfort whereas *gemütlich* (see **A**) refers to the atmosphere.

C *Verbringen* is always used for spending time; use *ausgeben* for money.

D *So gegen* is impressively colloquial and simple to remember.

E Use the verb *frühstücken* rather than *Frühstück haben*.

3 How the grammar works (page 12)

Q1

A Wir haben eine sehr gemütliche Küche, wo wir immer essen.

B Ich habe einen Schrank mit vielen Kassetten drin.

C Ich gehe in die Küche und frühstücke mit meiner Schwester.

D Ich stehe gewöhnlich um halb sieben auf.

E Ich ziehe mir die Schuhe an.

Comments

A Remember that the verb goes to the end in this subordinate clause after *wo*.

B Dative endings after *mit*.

C *in* + accusative shows movement; *mit* + dative.

D The verb is separable.

E The verb is both separable and reflexive.

Q2

A We have no garden.

B I have toast and jam for breakfast.

C I leave home at half past seven.

D I have three brothers and sisters.

Comments

A Watch out for the *kein/klein* trap!

B *Marmelade* is a 'false friend'.

C Remember that *verlassen* must have a place mentioned after it.

D The most obvious of 'false friends'.

UNIT 3: ESSEN UND GESUNDHEIT
1 What you need to know (page 15)
Q1

A Haben Sie einen Tisch für sechs am Fenster, bitte?

B Ich möchte die Speisekarte, bitte.

C Zweimal Bratwurst und Pommes Frites.

D Ein Glas Weißwein und ein Kännchen Tee, bitte.

E Zahlen, bitte.

Comments

This is the usual sort of role-play which you are expected to be able to conduct in a restaurant. You should get used to interpreting what you are required to do by following the sequence of pictures or diagrams.

Don't forget that the examiner – in this case the waiter – is part of the dialogue. He may go along with everything you say, but he may offer you alternatives, or indeed say that you can't have what you are asking for. Look at the examiner as he/she speaks, so that you become aware of any problems you need to deal with.

Q2

A Ich habe eine Magenverstimmung.

B Seit drei Tagen.

C Nein, aber mir ist heiß.

D Wie oft muss ich es einnehmen?

Comments

B German uses *seit* with the present tense to convey the English idea 'I have had it for three days'.

C Resist the temptation to say *Ich bin heiß*.

D Use *es* for *das Mittel*.

2 Higher vocabulary (page 16)
Q1

A Herr Ober, es fehlt ein Messer.

B … die Gabel ist nicht sauber.

C … der Kaffee ist kalt.

D Meine Freundin ist auf der Straße hingefallen.

E Sie hat sich am Bein verletzt.

Comments

Avoid direct translation of the sentences in front of you.

A *Fehlen* is the usual way of saying something is missing. You might add *mir* after *es fehlt*.

B No need to say *meine Gabel*; the definite article is quite sufficient.

C Similar to **B**.

D *auf* not *in*; *hingefallen* not simply *gefallen*.

E The reflexive *sich verletzen* requires you to say where the injury is: *am Arm, am Fuß*, etc.

3 How the grammar works (page 18)

Q1

grapes _Trauben_	school subjects _(das Fach)_ _Schulfächer_
peas _Erbsen_	school books _Schulbücher_
carrots _Karotten_	exercise books _(das Heft)_ _Hefte_
potatoes _Kartoffeln_	friends (masc.) _(der Freund)_ _Freunde_
drinks _Getränke_	
trousers _eine Hose_ (sing.)	friends (fem.) _(die Freundin)_ _Freundinnen_
shoes _Schuhe_	3 pounds (weight) _3 Pfund_ (not plural)
socks _Socken_	2 kilos _2 Kilo_
glasses _eine Brille_ (sing.)	teeth _Zähne_
buses _Busse_	fingers _Finger_ (plural = sing.)
	feet _Füße_

Comments

Just as in English, the definite article is not always required; indeed it sometimes makes nonsense of the sentence. If you say _Ich mag die Bohnen_, it implies that the listener knows which beans you are talking about. Perhaps you simply mean _Ich mag Bohnen_, which implies that you like beans in general. Think carefully before using _die_, every time you use a noun in the plural.

Q2

A Welches Auto ist schneller, dieses oder jenes?
B Jedes Mädchen mag diese Popgruppe.
C Ich mag diese Schuhe nicht. Welche magst du?
D Jeder weiß die Antwort.

Comments

A _Jenes_ is almost always used to contrast with _dieser_. However, _dieser_ is frequently used to mean 'that' on its own, even when the article or person in question is not close at hand.
B Don't forget: **das** Mädchen. **She** is not feminine!
D Unless there is a clear reason to use another gender, for instance, in a class of girls, we assume that 'everyone/everybody' is masculine.

UNIT 4: ICH, FAMILIE UND FREUNDE

1 What you need to know (page 21)

Q1

A Ich komme mit meinen Großeltern gut aus.
B Meine Brüder und ich verstehen uns nicht sehr gut.
C Meine Tante arbeitet bei Waitrose/im Supermarkt.
D Meine Mutter hat keine Geschwister. Sie ist Einzelkind.
E Meine Schwester und ich interessieren uns für Vögel.

Comments

A/B Decide which of the phrases you can best remember. One contains a separable verb, the other a reflexive verb. You need to master one of them; you are bound to need it in the Speaking Test.
C Both _bei_ and _im_ can mean 'at' and 'at the'.
D Remember that _Geschwister_ means 'brothers and sisters'. It is frequently mistaken for _Schwester_.
E If you have difficulty with the reflexive pronoun, look back to Unit 2.

Q2

Ich heiße Charles.
Meine Schwester Mary ist verheiratet und hat drei Kinder.
Meine zwei Nichten heißen Ann und Melissa, und mein Neffe heißt Tom.
Ich komme mit meinem Schwager Bill sehr gut aus.
Meine Eltern, James und Alice, sind sehr tolerant, und ich verstehe mich gut mit ihnen.

Comments
You can combine the information on the family tree in a number of different ways. Try to make these family descriptions interesting by the addition of adjectives and short pieces of additional information such as interests. You will learn more about these in the next unit.

2 Higher vocabulary (page 22)

Q1

Ich bekomme kein Taschengeld, aber ich arbeite nach der Schule im Supermarkt – zwei Stunden pro Tag. Ich verdiene fünfzig Pfund die Woche und ich spare das Geld für ein Motorrad. Ich gebe auch am Wochenende ein bisschen aus, entweder für eine Zeitschrift oder für das Kino.

Comments
Try the first sentence again. Use a *weil*... clause instead of *aber*, and remember to do the subject/verb inversion after it. The rest of what you can say arises out of your own experience, so make sure you check the vocabulary with your teacher well in advance. Don't try to ask 'What's the German for "newsagent"?' in the exam room! *Entweder*... is always worth adding to *oder*... It does show more control and style.

3 How the grammar works (page 24)

Q1

A höher
B später als
C lieber
D besser
E dreckiger

Comments

A/B Because a direct comparison is being made with other people, the comparative plus *als* is needed in both sentences.

C You can create interest in your Speaking Test by showing your preferences, not simply your likes and dislikes.

D The superlative is also possible, because it implies that you have looked at more than the two jackets.

E *Noch* almost always introduces the comparative – 'even bigger', even faster'.

Q2

A Mein ältester Bruder spielt Volleyball öfter als ich.
B Die meisten Schüler in der Klasse laufen schneller als ich.
C Das leichteste Schulfach ist Englisch.
D Ich finde Technologie am schwersten.
E Meine Schwester findet Englisch (genau) so schwer wie Technologie.

Comments

A The adjective needs *-est* plus the masculine ending *-er*.

B *Die meisten* translates as 'most of the' and is very common.

C You might also use *einfachste*.

D *Das Schwerste* is also possible here.

E *Genauso* is written as one word in phrases such as *Ich bin genauso gut wie du!*

UNIT 5: FREIZEIT UND FERIEN

1 What you need to know (page 26)

Q1

For example:
A Ich sehe gern fern.
B Ich gehe einmal im Monat ins Kino.
C Ich treffe mich am Wochenende mit meinen Freunden.
D Ich spiele gern Volleyball.
E Ich lese gern Romane.

Comments

A Remember to separate the verb (see Unit 2).

B Frequency (per week/per month) is expressed either by *pro* or *in*: *einmal pro Woche, zweimal im Jahr*.

C Note the reflexive verb *sich treffen*.

D/E Add *gern* to the present tense of the verb to express liking.

Q2

For example:

A Es gibt zwei Discos und einen Jugendklub.

B Das nächste Hallenbad ist zwei Kilometer von zu Hause entfernt.

C Der Eintritt kostet zwei Pfund fünfzig.

D Ich spiele kein Instrument – aber ich höre gern Musik.

E Ich arbeite in einem Supermarkt/in einem Schuhladen.

Comments

A Be prepared to say more than one item.

B *Von ... entfernt* means 'away from'.

C Don't forget to say the price in pounds, not euros.

D Use the question to lead into something you do like.

E Don't forget to use *in einem* not *im* here, because the examiner doesn't know which shop you are talking about.

2 Higher vocabulary (page 28)

Q1

1+2+4 In den letzten Osterferien war ich mit meinen Freunden in Schottland. Das ist das erste Mal, das wir nach Schottland gefahren sind.

3 Wir sind mit der Bahn dahin gefahren, aber ich fand die Fahrt ziemlich lang.

5 Wir sind in einer Jugendherberge in einem Dorf geblieben. Es war sehr preiswert aber die Betten waren unbequem.

6+7 Das Wetter war die ganze Woche schön und wir haben einen Ausflug an die Küste gemacht. Wir haben auch ein Schloss und ein Automuseum besucht.

8 Meine Freunde fanden das Schloss schön, aber ich fand das Automuseum interessanter. Die Landschaft in Schottland ist herrlich, finde ich.

Comments

This is a 'bread and butter' answer at this level. You should be able to do a number of variations around this model, changing the weather, the places you visit and how you felt about them.

For the A and A★ candidates it is necessary to add a problem or difficulty which you can then overcome.
For example:
- You lose your wallet and go to the police station to report it.
- You get soaking wet in a summer storm and have to get changed.
- The car breaks down and you have to wait for the garage to fix it.

The vocabulary for these different areas appears in other units.

3 How the grammar works (page 30)

Q1

A Ich komme mit dem Rad.

B Ich gehe zu dem/zum Markt.

C Ich kaufe es für meinen Freund.

D Der Park liegt gegenüber der Bank.

E Ich fahre in die Stadt.

Comments

A Most forms of transport use *mit*. *Zu Fuß* is a common exception.

B Try to use the common contractions where possible: *am/ans, beim, im/ins, vom, zum/zur*.

C The possessive adjective follows the pattern of the indefinite article *ein*.

D Nowadays, *gegenüber* is increasingly found in front of the noun, but still follows pronouns: *er stand mir gegenüber*.

E This is such a common phrase that you could learn to add another simple one before it for the transport – *mit dem Bus, mit dem Rad*.

Q2

A um das Haus

B im Theater

C ins Esszimmer

D von der Schule

E aus dem Fenster

Comments

A *Um* is always used with the accusative, whether or not there is movement implied.

B 'We will **go to** the theatre, but we will **be in** the theatre when we meet' – no movement, therefore dative.

C 'Where did we take the plates?' – movement is obviously implied, so accusative.

D Even though there is movement, *von* is **only** used with the dative.

E Similarly with *aus*, despite the obvious movement.

UNIT 6: FREUNDE UND GESELLIGKEIT

I What you need to know (page 32)

QI

A Tschüss!
B Gute Reise!
C Quatsch!
D gestern
E Schade!

Comments

A All the rest are greetings you use when you meet.

B You would use the others at mealtimes.

C You would use the others to wish people a good time.

D The other expressions are for making arrangements in the future.

E The other exclamations are happy and positive.

Q2

Suggested dialogue:

Anton: **Servus!**
Bodo: Hallo Anton!
Anton: **Wie geht's dir?**
Bodo: Ganz gut, danke. Und dir?
Anton: **Mir geht's ausgezeichnet, danke.**
Bodo: Darf ich meinen Vetter Hans vorstellen?
Anton: **Es freut mich, dich kennen zu lernen. Wo kommst du denn her?**
Hans: Ich komme aus Dresden. Ich bin schon seit einer Woche hier.

Anton: Wann wollen wir ins Kino gehen?
Bodo: **Ich weiß nicht. Es ist mir egal.**
Anton: Dann sagen wir Montag gegen acht Uhr.
Bodo: OK. **Bis dann.** Tschüss!

Comments

- Although *Servus* is often regarded as regional, you must not be surprised to hear it in any area of Germany. People do move house, after all!

- Notice that the *du* form is most common among teenagers, even when meeting for the first time. You can keep the *Sie* form for meeting older people you don't know or for formal situations, such as at the doctor's, or when talking to your teacher.

- *Ich komme aus* tells people where you live, i.e. originate from. *Ich komme vom Arzt, von der Schule* tells someone where you have come from, i.e. where you have just been.

- Anton uses *Wann wollen wir…?* to ask 'When shall we…?', but don't forget that you should usually use *werden* to introduce a future idea. (See Unit 10 for more examples of the future tense.)

2 Higher vocabulary (page 33)

QI

A Wie wäre es mit einem Tennisspiel? Hast du Lust, Tennis zu spielen?

B Wollen wir nicht lieber zum Strand (gehen)?

C Ich habe keine Lust, ins Schwimmbad zu gehen.

D Könnten Sie bitte Ihre Familienname buchstabieren bitte?

E Entschuldigen Sie bitte; ich habe Ihre Frage nicht verstanden.

Comments

The first three are just the sort of language you will often need in the oral examination. For example, 'Suggest to your exchange partner what you might like to do today.' 'Say you don't want to do that and suggest something else.'

C To go swimming you need to go *ins Schwimmbad*, although *Wie komme ich zum Schwimmbad?* is correct for asking directions and will take you to the place.

D You may also pose the question *Wie schreibt man das?* to achieve the same result.

D and E are for use in formal situations, perhaps on the telephone (**D**) or in the bank (**E**). There is little variation possible.

3 How the grammar works (page 35)

Q1
A weil
B bis, *or possibly* obgleich/obwohl
C damit
D sobald/wenn, *or possibly* obgleich/obwohl
E wenn/sobald

Comments
C Beware of using *so dass* as often as you would use 'so that' in English. Make sure you can tell the difference between the clauses which imply result and those which imply intent.

D/E *Wenn* would imply the conditional 'if', whereas *sobald* implies that the action in the following clause is bound to happen.

Q2
A Weil es stark regnet, gehen wir auf keinen Fall spazieren.
B Sobald meine Freundin vorbeikommt, können wir zusammen schwimmen gehen.
C Peter besucht morgen seine Großeltern, obwohl er zu Fuß gehen muss.
D Ich bleibe morgen mit meinem Bruder zu Hause, denn meine Mutter muss arbeiten.
E Meine Eltern kommen uns abholen, nachdem sie von der Stadt zurückkommen.

Unused:
1 ...weil sie kein Geld hat.
3 ...ist es sehr sonnig.

Comments
Apart from making the best sense of the sentences, the following might have helped you to put the clauses together:

A and B both began with subordinating conjunctions and you therefore had to create the 'verb, verb' pattern in the middle of the sentence. Only **3**, **5** and **7** could do this.
C, D and E began with main clauses and needed either another main clause or a subordinate clause to complete them. **1**, **2**, **4** and **6** could do this.

Unit 7: Die Stadt, Die Umgebung, Das Wetter
1 What you need to know (page 37)

Q1
A Ich wohne in einer großen Stadt im Nordosten.
B Es ist ein bisschen dreckig, aber ganz angenehm.
C Es gibt immer viel zu tun.
D Das Dorf ist ziemlich weit von der nächsten Stadt.
E Es gibt viel Sehenswertes in der Umgebung.

Comments
A Notice the difference between this and *in einer Großstadt* – 'in a city'.
B Compare two aspects of the town using *aber* between the adjectives.
C You could also use *es gibt immer etwas los* – 'there's always something on'.
D Notice that *weit* is all you need for 'a long way'.
E *Sehenswertes* means 'things/places worth seeing' or simply 'sights'.

Q2
A Morgen wird es kalt und wolkig sein.
B Das Wetter ist heiter, wenn auch etwas kühl.
C Der Wind kommt aus dem Norden, und es friert.
D Es ist ganz nass und ziemlich neblig.
E Die Tiefsttemperaturen liegen bei 5 Grad.

Comments

A You can use *bewölkt* for *wolkig*.

B *Wenn auch* is a stylish way to make a contrast.

C Compare this with 'I come from...' (*Ich komme aus...*).

D Qualify the adjectives wherever possible.

E *Liegen bei* is the weather jargon for 'will be around'.

2 Higher vocabulary (page 38)

Q1

A Ich wohne gern in Keld, weil die Landschaft (in der Umgebung) so herrlich ist.

B Man kann in der Umgebung schön spazieren gehen.

C Das Dorf hat weder Disco noch Jugendklub.

D Man kann mit dem Bus in die nächste Stadt fahren, aber ich finde die Disco dort nicht so gut.

E Man sollte dort ein Sportzentrum bauen.

Comments

You should be on very firm ground in this whole topic area. You have worked out what you want to say about your own town or district, without moving into areas of difficult vocabulary.

A *Schön* is so over-used that the examiner will undoubtedly rejoice to hear an alternative! Try *hervorragend*, *wunderschön* and *ausgezeichnet* for variations.

B Here *schön* is used to qualify *spazieren* and gives you just the meaning you need. It is much more elegant than *einen schönen Spaziergang machen*.

C *Weder... noch...* is essential for those higher grade marks.

D Remember to add your opinion at this level. As simple as it may sound, it is what the examiner needs to hear in order to put you in the Higher bracket of candidate.

E Contrast the use of *man* here and in sentence **D**.

3 How the grammar works (page 40)

Q1

Time	Manner	Place
gestern	mit meiner Mutter	in die Stadt
um 8 Uhr	zu Fuß	auf der Hauptstraße
früh am morgen	relativ billig	hinter dem Rathaus
dann	mit vollen Taschen	zum Markt
gegen 1 Uhr		zum Auto

Comments

You should build up a list of useful phrases like these, which you can use in a number of different situations. These are particularly good for 'filling', when you check back through your work and find you are 15–20 words short of the required total.

Q2

For example:

A Ich habe die Jacke gestern mit meinem eigenen Geld gekauft.

B Wir sind letztes Jahr mit der ganzen Familie nach Portugal gereist.

C Bringen Sie das Buch sofort zu Ihrem Mathelehrer!

D Sie kommt morgen nach der Schule ins Kino mit.

E Wir können nächste Woche nicht in Urlaub fahren.

Comments

D Don't be misled by *nach der Schule*, which means 'after school' and so is a time phrase.

E The position of *nicht* can of course vary according to the meaning you want. For example, *Wir können nicht nächste Woche in Urlaub fahren* would imply that you could go some time other than next week.

Unit 8: Einkaufen
1 What you need to know (page 42)

Q1

For example:

A Ich möchte eine Tube Zahnpasta.
B Geben Sie mir ein Kilo Äpfel, bitte.
C Haben Sie ein Paket Waschpulver, bitte?
D Und dann hätte ich gern fünf Scheiben Schinken.
E Ich möchte eine Flasche Limonade, bitte.

> **Comments**
>
> Notice that there are at least four ways of asking for something when shopping. Make sure that you can use at least one of them successfully every time without a second thought. You will recognise the others, but you don't have to alternate them. After all, you probably stick to the same phrase in English all the time.
>
> **D** This turn of phrase is for the second or third thing you are asking for.

Q2

A Haben Sie das gleiche in Blau?
B Das ist mir zu teuer. Haben Sie etwas Billigeres?
C Das ist mir zu groß. Haben Sie eine Nummer kleiner?
D Ich suche etwas für meinen Vater.
E Können Sie es bitte als Geschenk einpacken?

> **Comments**
>
> **A** Change the gender of *das gleiche* according to the garment.
> **B** The word following *etwas* must be a noun and therefore has a capital.
> **C** Notice the addition of *mir* in both **B** and **C**. Use *Nummer* not *Größe* for 'size' in this context.
> **E** Notice the alternative place for *bitte*, instead of leaving it to the end.

2 Higher vocabulary (page 43)

Q1

A Könn(t)en Sie (mir) einen Hunderteuroschein wechseln, bitte?
B Kann ich hier Geld wechseln, bitte?
C Kann meine Mutter mit Kreditkarte bezahlen?
D Was kostet dieses Paket nach England?
E Ich möchte fünf Briefmarken zu 51 Cent, bitte.

> **Comments**
>
> **A** *Können* is simpler, but the subjunctive *könnten* is more polite. *Mir* adds the idea of 'for me' and would be a stylish addition.
> **B** Note the position of *hier*.
> **C** *Darf meine Mutter...* would also be usual.
> **D** *Wie viel* is also usual.
> **E** *Kann ich ... haben* is equally acceptable.

3 How the grammar works (page 45)

Q1

Mein jünger**er** Bruder lief durch die offen**e** Tür des groß**en**, weiß**en** Gebäude**s** und kaufte eine einfach**e** Fahrkarte nach Bonn. Mit den beid**en** Koffer**n** in den Händen ging er den lang**en** Bahnsteig entlang, bis er den letzt**en** Wagen erreichte. Peter fand ein leer**es** Abteil und legte die schwer**en** Koffer in das altmodisch**e** Gepäcknetz über dem einzig**en** frei**en** Platz im ganz**en** Zug.

> **Comments**
>
> | | Case required | Function |
> |---|---|---|
> | 1 | masculine nominative | subject |
> | 2 | feminine accusative | following *durch* |
> | 3 | neuter genitive | possessive |
> | 4 | neuter genitive | possessive |
> | 5 | neuter genitive | (Remember to add −s to the noun.) |
> | 6 | feminine accusative | direct object |
> | 7 | dative plural | following *mit* |
> | 8 | dative plural | (Remember to add −n to the noun.) |
> | 9 | masculine accusative | to agree with the *entlang* following it |
> | 10 | masculine accusative | direct object |
> | 11 | neuter accusative | direct object |
> | 12 | plural accusative | direct object |
> | 13 | neuter accusative | following *in* |
> | 14 | masculine dative | following *über* |
> | 15 | masculine dative | following *im* |

CHECK YOURSELF ANSWERS

Q2

A Unser VW ist jetzt sehr **alt**. Vater möchte einen **modernen** Wagen kaufen.

B Ich kaufe mir eine **neue** Jacke; die **alte** kann ich nicht mehr anziehen.

C Der **letzte** Bus war zu voll, aber der **nächste** kommt in fünf Minuten.

D Die Hose ist nicht in der **alten** Kommode, sondern im **neuen** Kleiderschrank.

E Du bist ein **nettes** Mädchen, aber mein **neues** Fahrrad leihe ich dir nicht!

Comments

A 1 no agreement after the noun;
2 masculine accusative

B 1 feminine accusative; 2 feminine accusative – noun omitted

C 1 masculine nominative; 2 masculine nominative – noun omitted

D 1 feminine dative; 2 masculine dative

E 1 neuter nominative – don't forget that girls are not feminine in German!
2 neuter accusative – and notice the different word order for emphasis.

UNIT 9: WIE KOMMT MAN DAHIN?

1 What you need to know (page 47)

Q1

A Gehen Sie an der Brücke vorbei, und dann nehmen Sie die dritte Straße rechts.

B Gehen Sie bis zur Ampel und dann biegen Sie nach links ab.

C Die Galerie liegt auf der linken Seite dem Rathaus gegenüber.

D Nehmen Sie die nächste Straße links und gehen Sie immer geradeaus.

E Sie können es nicht verfehlen.

Comments

These examples are straightforward and you should try to memorise them. Although you may feel you know the structures, make sure you are confident with the genders of all the places in the town, so that you can get the zum/zur and am/ an der, etc. correct every time.

C gegenüber dem Rathaus is also correct.

Q2

Stimme: Hier Fleischauer.

Sie: Wir haben eine **Panne**.

Stimme: Was ist denn los?

Sie: Wir haben ein **Problem** mit dem **Motor**. Können Sie einen **Mechaniker schicken**?

Stimme: Ja, aber nicht sofort.

Sie: Wie **lange dauert** es?

Stimme: Eine Stunde. Wo sind Sie?

Sie: Wir sind auf der **Autobahn** in der **Nähe** von Koblenz. Wir fahren **Richtung** Bonn.

Comments

This dialogue contains the key phrases to remember and is typical of the sort you may be expected to take part in for the Speaking Test role-play. The exam will not be testing your mechanical knowledge or skills, so you are unlikely to be asked to produce any specialist vocabulary.

2 Higher vocabulary (page 48)

Q1

• Es war ein schöner Samstagnachmittag. Ich lief die Landstraße entlang und überlegte, was ich in der Stadt kaufen wollte.

• Ein Freund ist mit dem Rad an mir vorbeigefahren, und hat 'Hallo' gerufen.

• Einen Augenblick später habe ich ein Auto hupen gehört und habe mich umgedreht.

• Das Auto ist mit dem Radfahrer zusammengestossen und dann gegen eine Mauer gefahren.

• Mein Freund ist glücklicherweise nicht schwer verletzt und sass neben seinem Rad auf dem Fußgängerweg.

• Ich habe sofort mein Handy aus der Tasche genommen und die Polizei angerufen.

Comments

This is an oral test and **not** an essay!
If you can say this much you will do very
well indeed!

The narration contains both imperfect and
perfect tenses. Remember that in spoken
narrative the imperfect tense is used for the
weather, your mood and continuous
happenings such as 'I was wondering what
to buy'. The perfect tense is needed for
single actions such as 'I turned round' and
'the car hit the cyclist'.

N.B. In a written story you will see and use
the imperfect tense more frequently.

Watch these more difficult separable verbs:
  an jemandem vorbeifahren - er ist an mir
  (dative) vorbeigefahren★
  sich umdrehen (reflexive) – ich habe mich
  umgedreht
  zusammenstossen mit + dative - es ist mit
  dem Rad zusammengestossen★

★These verbs take sein in the perfect tense.

3 How the grammar works (page 50)

Q1

A Ich habe **ihn** heute morgen nicht gesehen.
B **Er** hat **sie** getragen.
C Ich habe **sie ihm** gegeben.
D **Sie** schreibt **damit**.
E **Sie** ist mit **ihnen** in die Stadt gefahren.

Comments

A Masculine accusative
B Masculine nominative; feminine accusative
C Plural accusative; masculine dative – and
  notice the change in the word order!
D Feminine nominative; note that *mit + ihm*
  changes to *damit* for 'with it' (although
  mit ihm would be needed for 'with him').
E Feminine nominative; plural dative

Q2

A Die Frau, **die** den Wagen gefahren hat, war
  meine Nachbarin.
B Der Mann, **dessen** Auto es war, hat die
  Polizei angerufen.
C Die U-Bahn, mit **der** ich gefahren bin,
  hatte Verspätung.

D Die Kinder, **denen** ich die Bonbons gebe,
  sind meine Geschwister.
E Der Junge, **den** ich auf der Party traf,
  kommt aus meiner Klasse.

Comments

A Feminine nominative
B Masculine genitive
C Feminine dative after *mit*
D Plural dative
E Masculine accusative

UNIT 10: AUSBILDUNG UND BERUF
1 What you need to know (page 52)

Q1

A Mein Vater ist Mechaniker (von Beruf).
B Mein Bruder arbeitet als Krankenpfleger.
C Mein Onkel arbeitet bei Waitrose.
D Meine Kusine ist Lastwagenfahrerin.
E Unsere Nachbarin arbeitet selbstständig.

Comments

Make sure you know the jobs of people in
your family. Don't leave it until the day of
the exam. If you are unsure, or the job is
too complicated to describe in a single
word, then you must choose between
saying what he/she does in general terms
(e.g. *Er/Sie macht irgendetwas mit
Computern.*) or saying where he/she works
(e.g. *Er/Sie arbeitet im Büro/in einer Fabrik/
in einem Geschäft*). It would be too
embarrassing to say *Ich weiß nicht!*

Q2

A Bauer
B Verkäuferin
C Architekt
D Tierarzt
E Fußballspieler

Comments

A The others work in a shop.
B The others work in education.
C The others are manual occupations.
D The others work with people.
E The others work as creative artists.

2 Higher vocabulary (page 53)

Q1

For example:
Ich werde gleich arbeiten gehen. Ich habe eine Stelle in einem Büro.

ODER

Ich werde hier in der Schule bleiben. Ich mache Deutsch und Spanisch in der Oberstufe weiter.

ODER

Ich möchte auf die Berufsschule gehen, um einen Komputerkurs zu machen.

> **Comments**
>
> Give a reason for your choice. It can be made up, but it must sound convincing! It is unlikely that the examiner will follow up this line of questioning any further.
> For example:
> *Ich werde eine Stelle in einer Firma nehmen, **wo meine Tante arbeitet**.*
> *Ich lerne Fremdspachen, **weil ich später Journalist werden will**.*

3 How the grammar works (page 56)

Q1

A My brother is studying medicine at university.
B Our neighbour's son is doing an apprenticeship at Siemens.
C When do you have to start at college?
D Wouldn't you prefer to become a vet?
E How much will you earn as an apprentice?

> **Comments**
>
> **A** Note that the definite article is needed before *Universität*.
> **B** *Bei* is usually translated as 'at' or 'with'.
> **C** Note that the definite article is needed before *Berufsschule*.
> **D** Remember how to use *lieber*, the comparative of *gern*, to express preference.
> **E** Remember: the indefinite article is omitted before the name of a job in German.

Q2

A könnt
B musst
C darf
D soll
E Wollt

> **Comments**
>
> Modal auxiliary verbs will bring you a great deal of credit in both your Speaking and Writing Tests.

UNIT 11: AM ARBEITSPLATZ
1 What you need to know (page 58)

Q1

A Darf ich bitte Rudi sprechen?
B Können Sie Herrn Braun etwas ausrichten, bitte?
C Ich sage ihr sofort Bescheid.
D Möchten Sie lieber ein Fax schicken?
E Sie ist so gegen 2 wieder da.

> **Comments**
>
> **A** Notice that you do not need to put **mit** *Rudi*.
> **B** *Herr* adds an –n in all cases but the nominative.
> **C** *Bescheid* has no obvious translation here.
> **D** Remember how to use *gern*, *lieber* and *am liebsten* to add the meanings of 'like', 'prefer' and 'like most of all'.
> **E** So *gegen* gives a good approximation of time.

Q2

> **Bitte in Druckschrift schreiben**
> _____
> Familienname JENNINGS
> Vorname MARY
> geboren am 6 JUNI 1986
> _____
> **Familienstand**
> ledig/~~verheiratet/geschieden~~
> (bitte durchstreichen)
> Staatsangehörigkeit BRITISCH
> _____
> **Adresse**
> Straße HONEY END LANE
> Ort READING
> PLZ RG3 4EL
> _____
> Telefonisch zu erreichen? ja/~~nein~~
> tagsüber 0118 9596011
> abends 0118 9110959

Comments

The completion of your personal details is easy, but the official language of forms can sometimes be confusing. Although you will encounter this exercise as a writing test, it is much more a test of reading, and you need to have learned the specific vocabulary required on forms such as this one.

Note that in *Druckschrift schreiben* means you should write in capital letters.

2 Higher vocabulary (page 59)

Q1

A Sie sagt, dass sie heute nachmittag nicht kommen kann.

B Er hofft, dass wir morgen kommen können.

C Sie fragen, um wie viel Uhr wir ankommen werden.

D Ich habe ihn gefragt, ob das Auto in Ordnung ist.

E Er meint, dass wir so bald wie möglich kommen sollten [*OR* sollen].

Comments

Keep your eye on the subordinate word order in such sentences and don't forget the comma before the subordinate clause. You should be using the '*Neue Rechtschreibung*' now, so avoid writing *daß* even if you still see it in textbooks.

E Use *meinen* as often as you like when you want to convey that it is someone's opinion or suggestion, i.e. he thinks it would be a good idea if we come as soon as possible.

3 How the grammar works (page 60)

Q1

A Zeig' mir deine Hausaufgabe!

B Setz' dich hin!

C Holt eure Bücher 'raus!

D Schreibt das Datum!

E Macht weiter!

Comments

Now you have practised the regular verbs, check the handful of irregular ones.

Q2

Tom sagt, er kann erst um 8 Uhr nach Hause kommen. Er sagt, dass der nächste Bus um 7.50 Uhr ankommt. Er fragt, wann der Supermarkt schließt, und ob er etwas kaufen soll. Er sagt, dass er sehr müde ist.

Comments

This answer uses direct speech which in certain tenses can require you to use the subjunctive. This construction is best avoided at this level. Look in the Further Grammar section (page 128) for the few subjunctive uses which you need to recognise.

UNIT 12: AUSLAND UND TOURISMUS

1 What you need to know (page 62)

Q1

Wir **sind letzten** Sommer mit der **Bahn** nach Düsseldorf **gefahren**. Die Reise **dauerte** zehn **Stunden**.

Mein Freund und ich **haben Schlafplätze reserviert**, weil wir über Nacht **gefahren sind**. Wir **mussten** in Lille **umsteigen**. Wir **sind** gegen Mittag in Düsseldorf **angekommen**.

Comments

You should have been able to work out that you were travelling by rail, not by bus, because of the words *mit der...*, which needed to be followed by a feminine *Bahn*, not a masculine *Bus*. You should not have been tempted to put *geflogen* for the same reason.

The use of the modal *mussten* relieves the monotony of the perfect tense construction in every sentence. You might try introducing *wir konnten (nicht)* or *wir wollten* into parts of your journey description.

Q2

6 Wir sind um vier Uhr nachmittags in Bonn angekommen.

3 Ich bin ins Verkehrsamt gegangen.

8 Man hat uns ein preiswertes Hotel empfohlen.

5 Wir sind zum Hotel gefahren und haben in der Tiefgarage geparkt.

7 Wir haben uns gleich angemeldet.
2 Wir sind auf unsere Zimmer gegangen.
4 Ich habe mich geduscht und mich umgezogen.
1 Wir haben gegen sieben Uhr in der Pizzeria zu Abend gegessen.

Comments
Learning a simple account like this, with very few adverbs or adjectives, is just the sort of preparation which can be very useful for your Higher Level writing. From here, you can progress rapidly to double the word count by adding subordinate clauses and phrases about time, weather and mood.

2 Higher vocabulary (page 63)

Q1
A Die Kaufhäuser sind weltberühmt.
B Die Altstadt ist lebendiger als unsere Stadt.
C Das Verkehrssystem in der Stadt ist nicht so groß wie hier.
D Die Sehenswürdigkeiten sind viel interessanter als in (..........).
E Ich fand das Schloss ganz imponierend.

Comments
Remember the key comparisons (nicht) so groß wie and größer als. Speak positively about your experiences - real or imaginary - in the German-speaking town. Avoid finding everything langweilig! Toll, großartig and hervorragend make a much stronger impression.

3 How the grammar works (page 66)

Q1

vorbereiten	vorbereitet
anfangen	angefangen
überraschen	überrascht
einschlafen	eingeschlafen
aufstehen	aufgestanden
empfehlen	empfohlen
aufräumen	aufgeräumt
verkaufen	verkauft
vorschlagen	vorgeschlagen
erzählen	erzählt

Weak	
Separable	**Inseparable**
vorbereiten	überraschen
aufräumen	verkaufen
	erzählt

Strong	
Separable	**Inseparable**
anfangen	empfehlen
einschlafen	
aufstehen	
vorschlagen	

Comments
Of the weak verbs:
- *vorbereiten* needs no *ge* because of the inseparable prefix *be-*. This is tricky because the *vor-* is separable.
- *überraschen* and *verkaufen* similarly need no *ge-*.

Of the strong verbs, only *empfehlen* does not have a *ge-* because of its inseparable prefix.

Q2
A Ich war froh, dass ich **mein Portemonnaie gefunden hatte**.
B Mutti schien sehr böse, weil wir **uns verlaufen hatten**.
C Wir waren zufrieden, als wir **die Arbeit zu Ende geschrieben hatten**.
D Sie waren alle überrascht, nachdem meine Oma **die Geschichte erzählt hatte**.

Comments
Each of the main clauses in these sentences is in the imperfect tense because it describes someone's mood or feelings. This is a very good way to introduce the pluperfect in your narrative.

Unit 13: Die Welt

1 What you need to know (page 68)

Q1

A Meiner Meinung nach ist das Rauchen ungesund.

B Wir waren alle sehr schockiert über die Nachricht von einem Erdbeben in der Türkei.

C Der Hungersnot in Afrika scheint es kein Ende zu geben.

D Wir müssen mehr unternehmen, um die Umwelt zu schützen.

Comments

A *Meiner Meinung nach* is a stylish introduction to your opinion, as long as you remember to invert subject and verb afterwards.

B *Schockiert*, or perhaps even *erschüttert*, suggests a much stronger emotion than *überrascht*.

C/D Sadly, these two huge world problems seem unlikely to be solved very quickly, and you will need to be able to express an opinion about them, even if it sounds a little like a cliché.

---

3 How the grammar works (page 69)

Q1

A Manche freuen sich darüber; andere sind nicht zufrieden.

B Einige sind weggegangen, aber niemand hat sie gesehen.

C Es gibt nur wenig, was man machen kann.

D Jeder soll etwas machen, aber niemand hat Lust dazu.

E Welcher ist heute angekommen, dieser oder jener?

Comments

These pronouns must be committed to memory. They are all common and, most importantly, they are just the sort of small words which can change the entire meaning of a passage when you meet them in a comprehension test.

Unit 14: Exam practice Listening and responding
(pages 79–84)

☀ Section 1   Foundation

Transcripts

1   Also, Abendessen gibt es zwischen halb sieben und halb acht hier unten im großen Saal.

2   Wenn Sie abends länger ausbleiben wollen, sagen Sie uns Bescheid, und wir geben Ihnen einen Hausschlüssel.

3   Im Süden leichter bis mäßiger Wind aus dem Sudwesten, zeitweise Regen. Temperaturen zwischen 8 und 10 Grad.

4   Im Westen wird es wieder stark bewölkt.

5   Im Norden wieder trocken – heiter und sonnig. Höchsttemperaturen erreichen 14–16 Grad.

6   Im östlichen Gebieten leichter Wind aus dem Westen. Sonnig und warm. Temperaturen zwischen 14–16 Grad.

7   Wir wohnen fast an der Küste, wissen Sie, und ich treibe sehr gern Wassersport, besonders segeln.

8   Meine Damen und Herren, Sie haben bei diesem Rundgang durch die Stadt eine tolle Auswahl an Museen und Galerien. Wer sich für die moderne Kunst interessiert, kommt mit mir zusammen in die Gruppe 1, während Gruppe 2 das Heimatmuseum besucht. Falls Sie bei diesem Wetter lieber draußen sind, besucht die Gruppe 3 den botanischen Garten und die Parkanlage der Universität. Wir treffen uns wieder um 12.30 Uhr vor dem alten Rathaus und essen zu Mittag im Ratskeller.

9   Guten Tag! Können Sie bitte Herrn Blum eine Nachricht hinterlassen? Hier spricht Frau Tiegel: T-I-E-G-E-L. Können Sie ihm bitte sagen, dass ich erst um siebzehn Uhr kommen kann? Wir treffen uns wie geplant im Rathaus. Danke schön.

10   *Frank:*   Kommst du morgen mit zum Park? Wir wollen Rollschuh laufen.
   Birgit: Leider nicht. Meine Rollschuhe sind kaputt.
   Frank: Macht nichts, du kannst meine haben. Sie sind ganz neu. Ich trage die von meinem Bruder. Er braucht sie morgen nicht.

11   *Birgit:*   Ich weiß einfach nicht, was ich machen soll. Meine Noten in der Schule sind so schlecht, ich kriege andauernd Vieren.
   Frank: Das wird schon wieder gut werden. Vielleicht wenn wir den neuen Klassenlehrer bekommen.

Birgit: Und dann habe ich gerade mit meinem Freund Schluss gemacht. Ich habe einfach keine Lust auszugehen.

12 Unser Urlaub war ganz fantastisch. Wir haben einen Campingplatz gefunden – fast direkt am Meer. Und einen tollen Strand auch.

13 – Wir haben am Wochenende eine tolle Party bei uns zu Hause gehabt.
   – Was haben deine Eltern gesagt?
   – Nichts. Sie waren bei Freunden eingeladen und sind erst gegen Mitternacht nach Hause gekommen.

14 Also, dieser Platz an der Uni ist für mich ganz wichtig, wenn ich später mit Computern arbeiten will.

15 Doch, ins Ausland fahren können ist für mich sehr viel wert. Daher möchte ich Fremdsprachen weiterstudieren.

16 – Unser Sommerurlaub ist also fast ins Wasser gefallen.
   – Was ist denn alles passiert?
   – Der erste Campingplatz war total voll, und man hat morgens für eine Dusche Schlange stehen müssen. Das Meer war nicht weit, aber es waren dort nur Felsen. Der nächste Strand war ziemlich weit zu laufen. Also habe ich beschlossen, zum nächsten Campingplatz zu fahren, aber ich habe vorher nicht angerufen, und es war voll ausgebucht.

   Am Abend sind wir in einem Gasthaus an der Küste gelandet, wo wir zwei schöne Zimmer bekommen haben. Mit einem Blick aufs Meer, das war große Klasse. Und wir haben nicht selbst kochen müssen, denn das Essen dort war ausgezeichnet.
   – Also, Ende gut, alles gut.
   – Das kann man wohl sagen. Selbst das Wetter hat mitgemacht. Es war kein einziger Regentag in den vierzehn Tagen.

Answers

1	C	5	B
2	D	6	C
3	B	7	C
4	B	8	C + E

9

Lieber Herr **Blum**,

Frau **Tiegel** hat für Sie angerufen.
Sie kommt erst um **17** Uhr.
Treffpunkt: **Im** Rathaus

10 D

11 B

12 B

13 bei Freunden

14 Weil sie später mit Computern arbeiten möchte.

15 Weil sie gern ins Ausland fährt.

16 a It was very crowded./Queuing for a shower./There was no beach close by./The nearest beach was quite far to walk to.
  b To try another campsite.
  c That campsite was full, too.
  d They found good rooms with great views of the sea and good food. They had good weather all the time.

Examiner's comments

1 You have two times to understand for the mark; both phrases use the word *halb* which often proves tricky.

2 *Bescheid sagen* comes directly from the passage, but you might be distracted by the word *Schlüssel* which appears in two options.

3–6 These contain only standard weather vocabulary, nothing difficult, although you do not need all of it for the answers.

7 *Wassersport* is obvious, but which one? *Segeln* is one of the few sports which is not a cognate word, i.e. the same word as in English.

8 A must be discounted because one group is visiting a museum.
  B is tempting, but only two of the three groups are visiting these places.
  C is correct.
  D is tempting because you hear *Park* in another context.
  E is correct.

9 Two names to spell correctly, one time on the 24-hour clock and a wrong preposition. All crucial to the successful transmission of the message.

10 The intonation of Frank's speech will tell you how generous he is being, in offering Birgit his own new rollerskates.

11 Again you hear someone who is obviously 'down' about school, and about having finished with her boyfriend.

12 *Fast* is the key word. Almost directly by the sea is not directly by the sea. **C** and **D** will distract those who have not learned to discount the masculine *See* which means 'lake', as against the feminine *See* which does mean 'sea'.

13 This answer can be lifted from the text providing you have understood the preposition *bei* correctly.

14 The *warum* of the question really needs a *weil* to start the answer. Again the words are directly from the text.

15 Begin again with *weil* and watch the subordinate clause word order. You cannot, however, lift the answer from the text on this one.

16 *Voll* is very straightforward, but *Schlange stehen* is a bit more demanding. You would be unlikely to know *Felsen* (rocks), but *ziemlich weit zu laufen* should be easy enough.

  The word 'decide' leads you to the phrase following *beschlossen*, and *voll ausgebucht* again should present no problem.

  The three good things to come out of staying at the guest house have obvious positive words, like *schöne, große Klasse, ausgezeichnet*, and the comment about the weather – *kein Regentag* – is spelt out clearly.

Annas Stundenplan

Anna: Also, was ich in der Schule lerne?

Montag beginnt der Schultag nicht so gut – Englisch ist nicht mein bestes Fach, aber nach der Pause wird es schon besser, denn die Mathelehrerin ist ganz toll. Nach der zweiten Pause habe ich Deutsch, dann Informatik.

Dienstag ist auch nicht so schlecht. Erdkunde haben wir in der zweiten Stunde, das ist meist interessant, aber wir haben Deutsch zweimal an dem Tag, was ich gar nicht so toll finde. Turnen haben wir am Nachmittag, denn die Turnhalle ist sonst immer voll besetzt.

Mittwoch ist immer ganz lustig, denn nach der ersten Pause haben wir eine Doppelstunde Kochen.

Donnerstag haben wir drei Stunden mit unserem Klassenlehrer, Herrn Burger. Er unterrichtet Religion in der ersten, Geschichte in der vierten und Sozialkunde in der fünften Stunde. Glücklicherweise komme ich mit ihm gut aus.

Freitag haben wir eine Doppelstunde Sport. Das gefällt mir gut, weil wir meistens draußen spielen.

Ich finde es sowieso doof, Samstags in die Schule zu gehen, aber wir haben zumindest wieder Erdkunde in der ersten Stunde und eine Doppelstunde Technik, bevor wir nach Hause gehen.

Answers

You should have completed Anna's timetable as follows:

Stunde	Montag	Dienstag	Mittwoch	Donnerstag	Freitag	Samstag
I	Englisch	Deutsch	Mathe	Religion	Biologie	Erdkunde
2	Geschichte	Erdkunde	Deutsch	Englisch	Deutsch	Englisch
	P	A	U	S	E	
3	Mathe	Kunst	Kochen	Informatik	Sport	Technik
4	Musik	Physik	Kochen	Geschichte	Sport	Technik
	P	A	U	S	E	
5	Deutsch	Deutsch	Chemie	Sozialkunde	Englisch	
6	Informatik	Mathe	Latein	Mathe	Latein	
7		Turnen				
8		Turnen				

2 Transcript

Wie kommt man dahin?

 Die Andreaskirche
Gehen Sie hier geradeaus, über die Kreuzung. An der nächsten Kreuzung biegen Sie nach rechts. Gehen Sie am Rathaus vorbei bis zur nächsten Kreuzung. Die Andreaskirche liegt schräg gegenüber an der Ecke.

Der Bahnhof
Gehen Sie an der Kreuzung links und an der nächsten Kreuzung rechts. Gehen Sie geradeaus über die Ampel und der Bahnhof liegt auf der linken Seite nach etwa zweihundert Metern.

Das Einkaufszentrum
Gehen Sie hier gleich links und dann an der nächsten Kreuzung rechts. Das Einkaufszentrum liegt auf der linken Seite nach etwa hundert Metern.

Der Fernsehturm
Gehen Sie an der Kreuzung rechts, über die Brücke. Der Fernsehturm liegt auf der linken Seite nach etwa zweihundert Metern.

Das Kunstmuseum
Gehen Sie über die erste Kreuzung und biegen an der zweiten Kreuzung rechts ab. Sie laufen am Fluss entlang etwa zweihundert Meter, über die nächste Kreuzung und dann noch 'mal so weit, bis zur zweiten Kreuzung. Dort biegen Sie nach links ab, und das Kunstmuseum ist gleich auf der rechten Seite.

Das Malteserkrankenhaus
Gehen Sie hier geradeaus über die erste und die zweite Kreuzung. Sie gehen am Kreisverkehr immer weiter geradeaus und nehmen die erste Straße rechts. Das Malteserkrankenhaus ist das zweite Gebäude auf der linken Seite.

Das Rathaus
Sie gehen geradeaus über die erste Kreuzung und biegen an der zweiten Kreuzung nach rechts. Das Rathaus liegt auf der linken Seite nach etwa hundert Metern. Das können Sie gar nicht verfehlen.

Das Stadion

Hier an der Kreuzung rechts, und dann gehen Sie immer geradeaus über den Fluss und über die nächste Kreuzung. Das Stadion liegt links direkt am Fluss nach etwa hundert Metern.

Das Theater

Das Theater ist gar nicht weit. Hier an der Kreuzung rechts, über den Fluß und Sie sehen das Theatergebäude direkt nach der Brücke auf der rechten Seite.

Answers

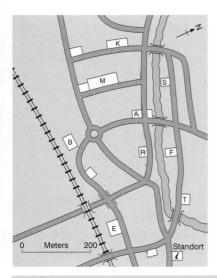

I Transcript

Im Fundbüro

Mann:	Guten Tag!
Mädchen:	Grüß Gott!
Mann:	Wie kann ich Ihnen helfen?
Mädchen:	Ich habe meine Jacke verloren.
Mann:	Wissen Sie, wann und wo Sie die Jacke verloren haben?
Mädchen:	Es war gestern nachmittag, nein, **gestern vormittag im Park**. Ich bin mit meinem Hund spazieren gegangen und ich habe eine Weile auf einer Bank in der Sonne gesessen. Aber dann musste ich ganz plötzlich meinem Hund hinterherlaufen. Und als ich ein paar Minuten später zurückgekommen bin, da war die Jacke weg.
Mann:	Können Sie die Jacke genau beschreiben?
Mädchen:	Es ist eine ziemlich alte Wildlederjacke, sie ist eigentlich **nicht viel wert**. Sie ist **hellbraun**, aber ziemlich schmutzig. Und es fehlt der obere Knopf.
Mann:	Und haben Sie außerdem etwas verloren?
Mädchen:	Leider ja. In der Innentasche waren meine **Hausschlüssel** und ein Portemonnaie mit etwa **zwanzig Mark** drin.
Mann:	Also, ich glaube, ich kann Ihnen in der einen Sache helfen. Eine solche Jacke ist heute morgen abgegeben worden. Man hat sie auf der Straße in der Nähe vom Park gefunden und gleich hierhergebracht.
[Pause]	
	Ist das Ihre Jacke?
Mädchen:	Ja, Gott sei Dank!
Mann:	**Aber das Geld und die Schlüssel waren nicht darin.** Es handelt sich in diesem Fall bestimmt um einen Diebstahl. Am besten informieren Sie gleich die Polizei. Und lassen Sie mir auch Ihre Adresse da, falls Ihre Sachen doch auftauchen.
Mädchen:	Danke für Ihre Hilfe. Ich gehe sofort zur Polizei.
Mann:	Es tut mir leid, aber Sie müssen noch zwei Mark Gebühr bezahlen.

Answers

1 Das Mädchen ging ins Fundbüro, **um etwas zu finden**.
2 Sie hatte die Jacke **am Tag davor im Park** verloren.
3 Die Jacke war **dreckig** und **nicht mehr neu**.
4 In der Tasche der Jacke hatte das Mädchen **ihre Schlüssel** und **etwas Geld**.
5 Das Mädchen hat **nur eine Sache** zurückgekriegt.

2 Transcript

 Ich heiße **Gerd**. In den Sommerferien bin ich fast jeden Tag **geritten**. Nur wenn das Wetter sehr schlecht war, bin ich zu Hause geblieben und habe **Musik gehört** oder **gelesen**.

Ich bin der **Martin**. In den Ferien habe ich wenig Zeit für Sport gehabt, weil ich den ganzen Tag im Supermarkt gearbeitet habe. Abends bin ich dann manchmal mit meiner Freundin entweder **ins Kino** oder **tanzen** gegangen. Das Geld, das ich verdient habe, spare ich für den **Skiurlaub** im Winter.

Hallo! Ich heiße **Jürgen**. Am Wochenende und in den Schulferien muss ich immer arbeiten, denn meine Hobbys sind etwas teuer. Ich habe mein **eigenes Pferd**, und bin so oft wie möglich mit ihm unterwegs. Im Winter **fahre** ich gerne **Ski**, denn wir wohnen nicht weit weg von Garmisch. **Radfahren** tue ich auch sehr viel, sonst kann ich hier auf dem Land meine Freunde nicht besuchen.

Hallo! Ich heiße **Peter**. Ich bin nicht sehr sportlich. Ich interessiere mich am meisten für **Popmusik** und ich **lese** auch sehr viel. Wenn ich mit meinen Freunden ausgehe, dann gehen wir meistens in die Stadt, vielleicht 'mal **ins Kino** oder in die Pizzeria.

Servus! Ich bin der **Norbert**. Hier in der Stadt zu wohnen ist für mich das Ideale. Die Disko ist hier an der Ecke, da geh' ich sehr oft hin. Und es gibt auch zwei **Kinos** gleich in der Nähe. Nur am Wochenende nehme ich ganz gern mein **Rennrad** und fahre aufs Land hinaus. Nur bei schönem Wetter natürlich.

Answers

Schreiben Sie die Namen	(skating)	(dinosaur picture)	(horse riding)	(open book)	(cycling)	(skiing)	(book & CD)
		✓	✓				✓
Martin	✓	✓				✓	
	✓			✓		✓	
Jürgen			✓		✓	✓	
Norbert	✓	✓			✓		
Gerd			✓	✓			✓
	✓				✓	✓	
Peter		✓		✓			✓

3 Transcript

Die Wettervorhersage

 Und jetzt die Wettervorhersage **für morgen, Samstag**, den 4. Oktober.

Zunächst bleibt das Wetter im gesamten Bundesgebiet wechselhaft,
wenn auch etwas wärmer als in den letzten Tagen.

In der Nacht zum Samstag meist bewölkt, zeitweise **Regen**. Im Süden
kann es zu einzelnen Gewittern kommen. Tiefsttemperaturen liegen
bei ein bis zwei Grad Celsius.

Morgen früh meist heiter und sonnig. **Frühtemperaturen vier bis
sechs Grad**. Im Laufe des Tages zunehmend wolkig, am Nachmittag
zieht ein atlantisches Tiefdruckgebiet nach Norden.

Im Süden teils sonnig, teils aber auch stark bewölkt und
Regenschauer. Tageshöchsttemperaturen liegen bei 12 Grad.

Im Norden wolkig, meist niederschlagsfrei. Tageshöchsttemperaturen
liegen bei 10 Grad. In den Nachmittags- und **Abendstunden** gibt es
zunehmend Schauer oder Gewitter.

Im ganzen Gebiet mäßiger, teils frischer Wind aus dem Südwesten.

Answers

1	Die Wettervorhersage kommt am Freitag im Radio.	✓
2	In den letzten Tagen war es etwas kälter als jetzt.	✓
3	Die erste Nacht bleibt trocken.	☐
4	Es wird am Samstag Eis auf den Straßen geben.	☐
5	Das Tiefdruckgebiet kommt vom Süden.	✓
6	Am Samstag sieht man im Süden keine Sonne.	☐
7	Am Samstagabend könnte es im Norden stürmisch werden.	✓
8	Es gibt fast keinen Wind.	☐

Examiner's comments

Weather forecasts are usually delivered quite quickly, and it is therefore essential that you recognise the key words straight away. This is where listening practice is easily within your grasp. If you do not have satellite or cable TV, simply tune in to a German radio station for a few minutes either side of the hour and try to catch a weather forecast. Have the vocabulary list at hand and check off the words as you recognise them. There are a number that are almost only heard in forecasts, so make sure you can spot them. The key words in this listening passage have been highlighted.

There are some aspects of the true/false questions that you should think about. It is unlikely that you will be offered exactly the same words in the tasks as are in the text. If the examiner wants you to answer *richtig*, the statement will almost certainly be re-worded from the original. For example:

1 The forecast is made on Friday for the following day, Saturday. Friday is not mentioned in the text at all, but you can easily infer it from the context.

Similarly, in **2** there is a reversed comparison. *It's getting warmer* implies that it has been colder in recent days. Therefore 'true' is the answer.

The statement **5** says that the low pressure system is moving northwards, so it is true to say that it is coming from the south.

The reference to *stürmisch* in **7** simply paraphrases the *zunehmende....Gewitter* in the passage.

The four wrong answers are almost exact opposites of what was said in the forecasts.

3 *trocken*; *Regen* in the passage.

4 *Eis auf der Straße*; *ein bis zwei Grad* in the passage.

6 *keine Sonne*; *Im Süden.... sonnig* in the passage.

8 *fast keinen Wind*; *frischer Wind* in the passage.

4 Transcript

Am Telefon

Ralf: Hallo, Bernd. Gehst du mit in den Park? Wir wollen alle Fußball spielen.

Bernd: Was! Bei diesem Wetter? Warte zumindest, bis der Regen aufhört. Dann gehe ich mit!

Ralf: Willst du heute abend mit ins Kino? Der neue James Bond Film läuft im Gangolf.

Bernd: OK. Aber erst nachdem ich meine Hausaufgaben gemacht habe. Sonst kriege ich Krach mit meiner Mutter.

Ralf: Und wann kann ich deinen 'Gameboy' ausleihen?

Bernd: Also jetzt noch nicht, aber bestimmt, bevor wir in Urlaub fahren. Bis dann behalte ich den.

Ralf: Und warum fahrt ihr jetzt schon in Urlaub? Wir haben erst im Juli Ferien.

Bernd: Mein Vater kann aber dann nicht mitfahren. Er bekommt keinen Urlaub in den Sommermonaten.

Ralf: Also.

Answers

1 Bernd will nicht gleich Fußball spielen, weil **es (im Moment) regnet**.
2 Er will mitgehen, wenn **es aufhört zu regnen/der Regen aufhört**.
3 Bernd geht ins Kino, nachdem **er seine Hausaufgaben macht/er seine Hausaufgaben gemacht hat**.
4 Ralf bekommt den 'Gameboy', bevor **Bernd in Urlaub fährt/Bernd wegfährt**.
5 Bernds Familie macht jetzt Urlaub, damit **sein Vater mitfahren kann/sein Vater auch Urlaub nehmen kann**.

> **Examiner's comments**
> The dialogue is relatively uncomplicated, but you need to complete the sentences with correct verbs and tenses.
>
> This type of exercise, where your answer is begun for you, steers you towards the right form of answer, but still makes you listen to the passage for the content. Whatever happens, don't simply write out verbs as you hear them. Once you have an idea what the answer is, check that you are using the correct form of the verb.
>
> - Sentence **1** needs only a simple *es regnet* to make it correct, but the sentences become progressively more difficult.
> - The two answers to **2** both require the use of the separable verb *aufhören*, with or without a verb to follow it.
> - Sentence **4** needs the idea of 'going away' to complete it; these are two straightforward possibilities.
> - Sentence **5** is more difficult to complete; the answer needs the modal verb *können* to make sense of it, but watch the word order carefully. The modal *kann* is the finite verb and must therefore come at the end of the clause.

Unit 15: Exam practice
Speaking (pages 95–7)

☀ Section 1 Foundation

1 Transcript of sample student's answers

Im Hotel

	Teacher:	Guten Tag. Kann ich Ihnen helfen?
	Student:	Ja. Wir möchten drei Zimmer, bitte.
	Teacher:	Für wie viele Personen?
	Student:	Zwei Erwachsene und vier Kinder.
	Teacher:	Möchten Sie Zimmer mit Bad?
	Student:	Nein, mit Dusche, bitte.
	Teacher:	Wie lange wollen Sie bleiben?
	Student:	Fünf Nächte, bitte.
	Teacher:	Geht in Ordnung.
	Student:	Was kostet das ingesamt?
	Teacher:	€474,00. Aber Sie brauchen noch nichts zu bezahlen.

Examiner's comments

At Foundation Level it is not always necessary to use a full sentence answer – a phrase will sometimes be sufficient. For the first and last utterances it would be difficult to avoid a sentence, however. *Drei Zimmer* to begin with would simply not be sufficient.

2 Transcript of sample student's answers

Im Café

	Teacher:	Guten Tag.
	Student:	Guten Tag.
	Teacher:	Was darf's sein?
	Student:	Einmal Bratwurst mit Pommes und ein Käsebrötchen, bitte.
	Teacher:	Und zu trinken?
	Student:	Ich hätte gern eine Limonade, und mein Freund möchte einen Kaffee.
	Teacher:	Einmal Limo, einmal Kaffee. In Ordnung.
	Student:	Wo sind die Toiletten, bitte?
	Teacher:	Hier gleich um die Ecke.
	Student:	Danke schön.

Examiner's comments

You should expect to start with a greeting every time. It certainly doesn't hurt to begin politely. The obvious *ich möchte* is omitted from the next utterance and this is perfectly acceptable, especially as the candidate goes on to use *ich hätte gern*. It is as well to have the two phrases ready, in order to avoid repetition. The last comment is obvious, but don't forget it!

ANSWERS AND TRANSCRIPTS
FOR QUESTIONS TO TRY

☼ Section 2 Foundation and Higher

1 Transcript of sample student's answer

In der Bank

Teacher: Was kann ich für Sie tun?
Student: Ich möchte Reiseschecks einlösen.
Teacher: Was für Reiseschecks haben Sie denn?
Student: Ich habe Sterling Reiseschecks, fünf mal Zwanzig Pfund.
Teacher: Wohnen Sie hier in Düsseldorf?
Student: Ich wohne bei einem Brieffreund in Bilk.
Teacher: Ach so. Darf ich Ihren Pass sehen?
Student: Leider nicht. Ich habe meinen Pass zu Hause gelassen.
Teacher: Dann kann ich Ihnen leider keine Schecks einlösen.
Es tut mir leid.
Student: Na gut. Bis wann haben Sie heute auf?
Teacher: Heute haben wir bis 18.30 Uhr auf.

Examiner's comments

The unpredictable element in this role-play is very easy, but remember to look at the examiner when you are expecting the question. Notice the use of the adverb *leider* for the idea of 'I'm sorry' when the candidate says he's left his passport at home. *Bis wann* is absolutely appropriate in his last utterance, but he could just as easily have asked *Wann machen Sie heute zu?*

2 Transcript of sample student's answer

Am Bahnhof

Teacher: Ja, bitte.
Student: Wann fährt der nächste Zug nach Bonn, bitte?
Teacher: Um 10.24 Uhr.
Student: Eine Rückfahrkarte nach Bonn, bitte.
Teacher: Um wie viel Uhr wollen Sie zurückfahren?
Student: Erst heute abend, so gegen 7 Uhr.
Teacher: In Ordnung, dann ist es etwas billiger.
Student: Muss ich umsteigen?
Teacher: Nein, der Zug fährt direkt durch.
Student: Ich danke Ihnen.

Examiner's comments

You may have learned *Einmal hin und zurück nach Bonn* and that would be fine, too, as a way of asking for a return ticket. Again, the unpredictable question is very simple. *So gegen 7 Uhr* is a stylish colloquial phrase, worth remembering as an alternative to *um*. If you forget *umsteigen*, you can of course ask *Fährt der Zug direkt (durch)?*

☼ Section 3 Higher

1 Transcript of sample student's answer

Teacher: Also, wie kann ich Ihnen helfen?

Student: Ich habe diese Hose gekauft und sie ist nicht in Ordnung.

Teacher: Was ist damit los?

Student: Die Hose ist gerissen. Hier, sehen Sie.

Teacher: Oh ja. Ich glaube, sie ist nicht richtig genäht worden. Wann haben Sie die Hose gekauft?

Student: Erst gestern. Ich habe sie noch gar nicht getragen. Was kann man machen?

Teacher: Ich gebe Ihnen gern das Geld zurück, oder Sie können sich eine neue Hose aussuchen. Was möchten Sie lieber machen?

Student: Ich hätte gern die gleiche Hose wieder in derselben Farbe.

Teacher: Mmm. Es tut mir leid. Wir haben diese Hose nur noch in Rot oder in Braun.

Student: Dann nehme ich sie in Rot, bitte.

Teacher: Gut. Und weil Sie zweimal fahren mussten, gebe ich Ihnen die Hose zu einem günstigen Preis.

Student: Danke schön. Das ist sehr nett von Ihnen. Auf Wiedersehen.

Examiner's comments

The difficulty with this sort of role-play is the constant need to stay 'on the ball', and concentrate on the unpredictable elements which come at you from the examiner. However, you should be able to think through many of the possibilities beforehand, which will cut down the unlimited nature of the exercise. You know, for example, that a shopkeeper is obliged to offer money back or exchange of goods in such a situation, so you can prepare for this choice. Similarly, you might guess that the shop might have no more of that particular article in stock. What do you do? And so on.

Taken at this level, the role-play is quite straightforward.

2 Transcript of sample student's answer

Teacher: Also, erzählen Sie mal etwas über die Deutschlandreise.

Student: Wir haben uns vor der Schule getroffen und sind schon um sieben Uhr in Reading abgefahren. Wir sind auf der M4 nach London und dann weiter über die Autobahn nach Dover gefahren.

Teacher: Und wann sind Sie dort angekommen?

Student: So gegen halb elf. Und dann mussten wir etwa eine halbe Stunde warten, bis wir auf den Zug fahren konnten. Wir sind also mit dem Shuttle durch den Tunnel gefahren. Wir fanden es alle ganz toll. Es war sehr interessant und ging ziemlich schnell. Wir sind schon um fünf vor zwölf in Frankreich aus dem Tunnel gekommen.

Teacher: Und was haben Sie die ganze Zeit im Bus gemacht?

Student: Wir haben uns gut unterhalten – Karten gespielt, Musik gehört und Witze erzählt. Die Lehrer waren alle gut gelaunt, und es war ganz lustig. Wir sind dann durch Nordfrankreich und Belgien nach Aachen weitergefahren, wo wir an einer Raststätte haltgemacht haben. Es war kurz vor drei Uhr. Dann haben wir zum ersten Mal Deutsch gehört.

Teacher: Und? Haben Sie etwas verstanden?

Student: Eigentlich, ja. Ich bin ins Restaurant gegangen und habe ziemlich viel verstanden. Dann waren es noch drei Stunden, bis wir in Düsseldorf angekommen sind. Die Gastfamilien haben schon vor der Schule auf uns gewartet.

Teacher: Was haben Sie dann gemacht?

Student: Wir haben uns natürlich begrüßt und sind mit dem Auto nach Hause gefahren. Wir haben zu Abend gegessen. Bratwurst mit Pommes. Ich hatte Hunger, und es hat gut geschmeckt. Dann habe ich nach Hause telefoniert und bin ins Bett gegangen. Ich war todmüde.

Teacher: Das glaube ich Ihnen. Es war ein langer Tag. Danke schön.

Examiner's comments

The candidate does the basics well and adds some stylish phrases to make a really good impression. For example, the first verbs are all straightforward and correct, but again, the addition of *so gegen* is very good to start the second phase of the narrative. The two modal verbs in the imperfect - *mussten* and *konnten* - are also worthy of merit, as are the other imperfect tenses in this section, which describe the feeling and mood.

The candidate's confidence is shown by the style in the next section – by not repeating *haben, haben, haben*, the verbs stand out even more. The mood of the teachers and the atmosphere of the coach are rightly in the imperfect. Then the long journey to Düsseldorf and the subsequent actions are covered by verbs in the perfect.

Don't be worried that you can't remember a piece as long as this. Your narrative may only need some of these features in order to convince the examiner of your competence.

☀ Presentation and Discussion

Transcript of sample student's Presentation

Teacher: Und worüber wollen Sie mir erzählen?

Student: Ich werde meine Familie beschreiben. Also, ich habe zwei Brüder und eine Schwester, die alle älter sind als ich. James ist schon 26 und Anthony is 22. Sie arbeiten beide bei Firmen in Southampton. Meine Schwester, Elizabeth, ist fünf Jahre älter als ich und arbeitet in der Bibliothek in der Stadt. Sie ist sehr glücklich dort, denn sie liest sehr gern.

Teacher: Und Ihre Eltern?

Student: Mein Vater ist gestorben, und meine Mutter arbeitet halbtags in einem Geschäft. Wir sind nur noch vier zu

Hause, denn mein ältester Bruder hat letztes Jahr geheiratet. Und meine Schwester will nächstes Jahr heiraten. Ich komme mit meinen Geschwistern sehr gut aus. Ich glaube, das kommt daher, dass ich so viel jünger bin. Wir haben uns nie um das Spielzeug gestritten, weil wir selten miteinander gespielt haben, als ich jünger war.

Teacher: Und wie kommen Sie mit Ihrer Mutter aus?

Student: Eigentlich ganz gut. Nur manchmal, wenn ich spät nach Hause komme, wird sie mit mir böse. Und das dauert auch nicht so lange. Meine Mutter ist ganz in Ordnung. Sie versteht viel Spaß und mag gern Witze. Ich glaube, wir sind überhaupt eine lustige Familie.

Wir wohnen in einem Zweifamilienhaus am Rande der Stadt. Ich wohne sehr gern hier, weil wir sehr nah am Wald sind. Ich habe als kleiner Junge sehr viel im Wald gespielt, und ich gehe immer noch gern dort spazieren.

Wir haben einen großen Garten und ziemlich viel Gemüse. Ich helfe meiner Mutter damit, denn es wäre für sie alleine zu viel Arbeit. Meine Schwester mäht den Rasen, und ich pflanze die Kartoffeln an. Es macht mir eigentlich Spaß im Garten zu arbeiten.

Teacher: Danke schön. Das war sehr interessant.

Examiner's comments

This candidate is well prepared, has covered the tenses required (the future is handled by *will*), and has demonstrated a good variety of structures. He uses *denn* several times, which allows him to continue with the simpler word order through the clauses. When he's talking about his brothers and sisters, the phrase *das kommt daher, dass...* is well prepared, as is the use of *sich streiten um....* The feelings and emotions are well handled, and the use of *es wäre* is also quite impressive at this level.

It is noticeable that the overall portrait of the family is a happy one. This leaves a positive impression on the examiner.

☼ General Conversation

Transcript of sample teacher's questions

- Wie viele Unterrichtsstunden gibt es hier an der Schule?
- Was sind Ihre Wahlfächer?
- Was wollen Sie nach der Schule machen?
- Wie groß ist Reading?
- Gibt es hier viel Industrie?
- Was gibt es zu sehen und zu tun in Reading?
- Was haben Sie letztes Wochenende gemacht?
- Wie helfen Sie normalerweise zu Hause?
- Was haben Sie nächstes Wochenende vor?

Transcript of sample student's Conversation

Teacher: Wie viele Unterrichtsstunden gibt es hier an der Schule?

Student: Es gibt fünf Stunden, jede Stunde ist 60 Minuten lang. Wir haben vier am Vormittag und eine am Nachmittag. Nach der zweiten Stunde gibt es eine kleine Pause von 20 Minuten.

Teacher: Was sind Ihre Wahlfächer?

Student: Geschichte, Erdkunde, Französisch - und Deutsch natürlich. Ich mag die Fremdsprachen besonders gern, weil ich gern reise.

Teacher: Was wollen Sie nach der Schule machen?

Student: Ich will zuerst Fremdsprachen studieren, vielleicht eine dritte Fremdsprache wie Russisch, zum Beispiel. Dann möchte ich eine Weile im Ausland arbeiten.

Teacher: Wie groß ist Reading?

Student: Die Stadt hat ungefähr hundertfünfzigtausend Einwohner, aber ich glaube, sie wird immer größer, denn man baut hier viele neue Siedlungen am Rande der Stadt.

Teacher: Gibt es hier viel Industrie?

Student: Nicht so viel. Es gibt viele Bürogebäude, aber weniger Fabriken. Viele Leute fahren auch jeden Tag nach London, um zu arbeiten.

Teacher: Was gibt es zu sehen und zu tun in Reading?

Student: Es gibt die Ruinen von der Abtei, die sehr berühmt sind. Und Reading liegt auch sehr schön an der Themse, also kann man schöne Dampferfahrten machen, aber so viel gibt es nicht für Touristen.

Teacher: Was haben Sie letztes Wochenende gemacht?

Student: Ich habe Hockey in der Schulmannschaft gespielt, und wir haben gewonnen, was sehr gut war. Und am Nachmittag habe ich meine Freundinnen in der Stadt getroffen, und wir haben zusammen einen Schaufensterbummel gemacht. Danach sind wir in die Pizzeria gegangen.

Teacher: Wie helfen Sie normalerweise zu Hause?

Student: Also, wir sind vier Kinder zu Hause, und jeder von uns hat seine Arbeiten zu machen. Ich decke den Tisch jeden Tag morgens und abends, und ich halte mein Schlafzimmer sauber.

Teacher: Was haben Sie nächstes Wochenende vor?

Student: Also, nächstes Wochenende ist etwas Besonderes. Wir werden eine Grillparty bei uns haben, denn mein Vater hat Geburtstag. Er wird vierzig. Wir haben viele Leute eingeladen, und viele seiner früheren Schulkameraden werden auch da sein.

Examiner's comments

Every question is answered fully here, with interesting details in many cases. It's clear that the candidate has prepared thoroughly and that none of the questions comes as a great surprise. This is as it should be. Much of the material is provided in earlier chapters of this book, and you will no doubt have practised similar language already with your teacher. When it is all put together like this, it makes a very strong impression of a competent candidate. There is more than enough material here to gain an A* Grade and you will not be expected to score all these points. However, you should make sure of at least some answers of this quality in order to assue yourself of the highest grade!

Unit 16: Exam practice
Reading and responding (pages 107–15)

☀ Section 1 Foundation

Answers

1 D   2 C   3 D
4 B   5 B   6 A
7 i) –; ii) ✓; iii) –; iv) ✓; v) –
8 B
9 i) B; ii) A; iii) B + F; iv) D; v) A

Examiner's comments
These Foundation Level questions are all straightforward multiple choice questions and should pose no problems.

☀ Section 2 Foundation and Higher

Answers

1 i) C; ii) F; iii) A; iv) E; v) B
2 i) Brieffreunde
  ii) über Weihnachten
  iii) hat keine Idee
  iv) ist nicht so gut in Bio
  v) sind gegen
  vi) weiterlernen

Examiner's comments
The small ads in Question 1 are a typical transition task to help you into the beginning of the Higher Level. The connection between the person and the appropriate advertisement is simple enough, but is not usually direct.
   In Question 2, the passage requires you to make a greater degree of deduction. It is self-evident from the whole letter that those involved are *Brieffreunde*, and it is fairly straightforward to infer that the *Winterurlaub* must have been in the Christmas holidays. (Don't forget that you need to know the German for Easter and Whitsun as well!) Questions iii) and iv) are paraphrases of the text, whereas v) is an attitude betrayed by what the parents say. *Biostudium anfangen* is simply expressed as *weiterlernen* for vi).

ANSWERS AND TRANSCRIPTS
FOR QUESTIONS TO TRY

☼ Section 3 Higher

Answers

1 **a)** ✓; **b)** –; **c)** –; **d)** ✓; **e)** ✓; **f)** ✓

Examiner's comments

Beware statistics! Don't begin to imagine what they might say when you read what the survey was about – they may have been designed especially for your exam! *Eine Umfrage* (which you have probably conducted at some time in your German classes) is simply a device for introducing opinions and preferences.

As mentioned elsewhere, you need not worry about your statistical competence when setting about these questions. Very little is asked of your maths skills except to recognise that 70% could be described as the majority a), or that 12% is more than 5% d). You can arrive at the answer for b) by two different methods: either by understanding the third sentence *Sie [Die Umfrage] zeigte auch...*, or by contrasting what young men used to want to do with their current ambitions. The third paragraph brings in the concept of job security for e) and the last paragraph gives an easy answer to f) in the word *flexible*. (Remember that this is *flexibel* normally, but drops one 'e' when it gains the adjective ending *-e*.)

2 **a)** D; **b)** J; **c)** H; **d)** C; **e)** E; **f)** G

Examiner's comments

The difficulty with such a passage is that you have longer descriptions of places to read and a small amount of overlap between all the charming, historical places with wonderful views or things to look at. However, the questions are crafted to eliminate certain of the options while directing your attention to others.

  a) *Das Weinstädtchen Königswinter* would be more appropriate than simply any other *Gaststätte*.
  b) The phrases *mittelalterliche Fachwerkhäuser* and *historische Gaststätten* give a fair indication where mother would be happy.
  c) *Spaß* is quite easy to spot but don't expect such information to be in chronological order when the exercise is multiple choice – for obvious reasons!
  d) Again the words *Gaststätte* and *herrlichen Ausblick* signal the answer.
  e) This is much more difficult because you need to realise that *des ersten Bundeskanzlers* puts you in the realms of history, even before you connect with *Museum*, which should confirm your choice.
  f) The word *weit* might draw you to the answer, contained in *ältere Leute ... herrlichen Gärten ... ohne weit gehen zu müssen.*

3 **a)** –; **b)** ✓; **c)** –; **d)** –; **e)** ✓; **f)** –; **g)** ✓; **h)** – **i)** – **j)** ✓

Examiner's comments

It is advisable to read the statements through first, before launching into the text. This way you may identify key words, usually nouns and verbs, which you hope to recognise in the text.

a) *Nach* not in den Osterferien.
b) This is a general comment and should be obvious.
c) *Für alle zehnten Klassen* is the phrase that tells you it's not for all classes.
d) You need to know that *ab der neunten Klasse* means 'from Class 9 onwards'.
e) This is almost the wording of the text.
f) This is an inference which you must work out from the text. Jürgen is clearly not worried about tests and exams.
g) *Leider* gives you the clue that Jürgen is not happy about Beate's situation.
h) *Schulfest*, not *Klassenfest*. Did you read it correctly?
i) Only *abends*.
j) Again, the word *genug* appears in the text to guide you.

Unit 17: Exam practice Writing (pages 122–5)

☼ Section 1 Foundation

I Sample student's answer

1	Zahnbürste
2	Hose
3	Pullover
4	Sportschuhe
5	Hemd
6	Geld
7	Badehose
8	Seife

Examiner's comments
These items of vocabulary should all be well within the 'safe' area for every candidate. This exercise is always intended as one in which every candidate should score maximum or near maximum marks.
Note:
● Do not use more than two full cognate words such as Pullover – these are the words which have identical spelling in both languages.
● Watch out for those which only differ by one or two letters, such as Kamera.

2 Sample student's answer

What do you do?	Where do you do it?
1 a Ich tanze.	**b** Im Jugendklub.
2 a Ich fahre Rad.	**b** Im Wald.
3 a Ich spiele Federball.	**b** Im Garten.

Examiner's comments
Spelling does count, but full sentences are not required. A short
phrase, as in the second column, is all that may be necessary.

3 Sample student's answer

- ■ Weather   Das Wetter ist toll hier in Schottland.
- ■ Activity   Heute fahren wir mit der Bahn nach Edinburgh.
- ■ Family   Wir wohnen alle bei meiner Tante.
- ■ Cinema   Ich werde mit meinem Bruder ins Kino gehen.
- ■ Meals   Heute abend gehen wir Pizza essen.
- ■ Shopping   Meine Mutter möchte neue Kleider kaufen.

Examiner's comments
It is not difficult to achieve the minimum 40 words if you write a short
sentence about each of the six items. The **communication** marks
are achieved by writing something intelligible about each key word.
The **accuracy** marks are basically for spelling.

✹ Section 2 Foundation and Higher

I Sample student's answer

Newbury, den 13. Mai

Liebe Gabi,

(Im Vergleich zu deiner scheint unsere Schule neuer zu sein, aber wir haben nur etwa fünfhundert Schüler und Schülerinnen.) Wir haben acht Unterrichtsstunden jeden Tag, aber wir sind den ganzen Tag in der Schule, weil wir viel später anfangen.

Ich komme zu Fuß in die Schule (und treffe mich so gegen 8.15 Uhr mit meinen Kameraden auf dem Schulhof). Die Schule beginnt mit einer Klassenversammlung um 8.40 Uhr (und die erste Stunde beginnt um neun Uhr).

Ich lerne (zwei Fremdsprachen, Französisch und Deutsch,) Franz seit vier und Deutsch seit drei Jahren. (Ich bin viel besser in Mathe als in den Wissenschaften, aber) mein Lieblingsfach ist trotzdem Sport. Ich habe letzte Woche in unserer Volleyballmannschaft gegen eine andere Schule gespielt. Wir haben gewonnen!

Nächstes Jahr werde ich Mathe und Englisch in der Oberstufe weitermachen.

Schreib bald,

deine Hannah

Examiner's comments

This is a relatively straightforward question and the better candidate need have no fear of writing such a short letter. It is, after all, much less than the same candidate will need to know for the speaking test. **However**, the skill to be learned here is to get as many good pieces of German into this short space as possible.

The following are items of language from the letter above that might impress the examiner favourably:

- *scheint ... zu sein* instead of the simple *ist*
- *Im Vergleich ... neuer* shows good use of the comparative
- Subordinate clause introduced by *weil*
- *Ich komme...* is a sentence containing **five** adverbial phrases in the correct order
- Correct use of *seit*
- *besser als* again shows good use of the comparative.

You must use the letter to show what you **can** do in German. This is a common topic and you must always expect it in your exam in some form or other. Remember: the information contained in your letter would equally impress your examiner in the speaking test.

You may now like to try writing your own letter, using the above sample and other material from earlier chapters.

2 Sample student's answer

Ich ging gerade am Park vorbei, als ich den Hund sah, der vor mir aus dem Park schoss und einen Ball über die Straße jagte. Der Wagen, der gerade die Straße entlang fuhr, musste scharf bremsen, und fuhr über den Gehweg, durch eine Mauer und in den Vordergarten eines Hauses.

Der Autofahrer stieg aus, schien nicht verletzt zu sein, und schaute sich seinen Wagen an. Der Vorderteil seines Autos war ziemlich kaputt, und ich glaube, er war außer sich vor Wut.

Dann kam ein Mann aus dem Park und über die Straße. Er lief mit der Leine in der Hand auf den Autofahrer zu und erklärte ihm, dass es sein Hund war, der den Unfall verursacht hat.

Dann kam der Hausbesitzer an. Er hatte geschlafen, sagte er, und wurde vom Lärm geweckt.

„Ich werde die Polizei anrufen" schimpfte er, und ging ins Haus zurück. In zwei Minuten war ein Streifenwagen da, und alle drei Leute redeten mit den zwei Polizisten.

(160 words)

Examiner's comments

Excellent. All the major points in the pictures are covered, as are the past and future tenses. In this case, the candidate has used the conventional imperfect tense very well, but he/she might equally have given the account in the perfect tense, remembering to leave feelings, circumstances, etc. in the imperfect.

What stands out about this passage is the extent to which the adverbial phrases tell the story; *aus dem Park, über die Straße*, etc. give plenty of detail. The opinion is expressed by *ich glaube*, and the expression that follows has been specially learned to replace the usual *böse*.

Notice that the speech is described in four different ways using *sagen, schimpfen, erklären* and *reden*. This makes a very strong impression on the examiner reading the script.

The pluperfect in *hatte geschlafen* and the passive in *wurde geweckt* are particularly welcome inclusions at this level.

This is undoubtedly at least a Grade A candidate.

INDEX